Remodeling with
TILE

By the Editors
of Sunset Books and
Sunset Magazine

Handmade Japanese tiles, 1-1/4" by 8-3/4", are randomly arranged on this exterior-to-interior entry wall for maximum effect. Half an inch thick, the tiles are set in staggered rows. Large 7" by 14" Japanese tiles in herringbone pattern bring floor into harmony with wall. Design: International Tile and Supply Corporation.

Lane Publishing Co., Menlo Park, California

Tile: Colorful, decorative . . . and practical

When you're remodeling or decorating and it's time to consider surfacing materials, tile should be near the top of your list; its qualities are hard to beat. Featured throughout this book are the three most common kinds of tile: ceramic, resilient, and wood.

Color photographs on the first 32 pages provide a sampling of ideas for the many uses of tile. The remainder of the book is a how-to-do-it guide—heavily illustrated with artwork—to help you choose, install, and care for the tile. Since there are so many kinds available commercially, always be sure to follow any specifications provided by the manufacturer of the tile you are using. This same advice applies to supplemental tiling materials such as adhesives and grouts.

For their help and contribution of information, we wish to thank American Olean Tile Company; Pauline Ammirata, Creative Ceramics; A. R. Andries, Floor Service Supply Co.; Hugh Barclay, Jr., Tilecraft Ltd.; Carl Brodsky, The Tile Shop; Pat Burr, Tile West, Inc.; Betty Busby, Gilbert & Chang; Faye Byrnes, Superior Home Center; Helen Colijn; Frank Eastus, Tile by Frank; Laurie Fox; Mike Gaines; Anne Gilbar; Darrel Gilmore, Color Tile; Johansen Tile Company; Elaine Sewell Jones; David Klages; Steve Lewis, Ceramic Tile Sales; Henry Loya, Nissan Tile Distributing Corp.; Gloria & Dan Malloy, International Tile and Supply; Dwight Marsh, Tileman; Bob McIntyre and Joe Taylor, McIntyre Tile; Paul McKim; Richard B. Morrall; Roland Negrini, Roma Tile Company; Chris Payne; Marvin Ravely, Color Tile Supermarts; Joan Spiers, Barbara Vantrease Beall Studio; Darrell Stuart, Stuart Floor Company; Deborah and Paul Sussman; and Donald W. Vandervort.

A special thank you to Emil te Groen, Northern California Ceramic Tile Industry, for so generously sharing his expertise and knowledge with us.

Choice of moisture-resistant flooring for this garden room was prompted by direct access to hot tub on adjacent outdoor deck. Slightly textured to prevent wet feet from slipping, 8″ hexagonal tile with matte glaze provides a functional solution. Architect: William B. Remick.

Supervising Editor: René Klein

Research and Text: **Jim Barrett**
Alyson Gonsalves
Don Rutherford
Mike Scofield
Diane Tapscott

Design: **Joe di Chiarro**

Illustrations: **Terrence Meagher**

Photographers: Armstrong Cork Company: 18 top right. **Edward Bigelow:** 1, 3, 6, 7, 8, 9, 10, 11, 12, 13, 15 top left, 16, 17, 18 bottom left, 20, 22 right, 23 top and bottom left, 24 top, 25 top, 26, 27 bottom, 28 left, 29 right, 30, 31 bottom. **Color Tile Supermart, Inc.:** 14 top, 27 top, **Steve Marley:** 4-5, 14 bottom, 15 bottom left and right, 18 top left, 19, 21, 22 left, 23 bottom right, 24 bottom, 25 bottom left and right, 28 right, 29 left, 31 top, 32, 34, 36, 37, 39. **Norman A. Plate:** 2.

Cover: Two of the basic tiles in a kitchen situation: red ceramic countertop contrasts pleasingly with vinyl floor tiles. Design: William B. Remick. Photograph: Norman A. Plate.

Editor, Sunset Books: David E. Clark

Eighth printing October 1985

CONTENTS

Custom painted and glazed, these 6″ by 6″ tiles with garland pattern beautify both the fireplace opening and the hearth. This installation is a good weekend project for the conscientious do-it-yourselfer. Tile design: Barbara Vantrease Beall Studio.

TILE IN COLOR

. . . ceramic, resilient, and wood

It's sort of magic, the way in which tile adapts itself so easily to every style and taste. You can match any mood, create any kind of appearance; merely choose among the hundreds, even thousands, of tile designs, textures, sizes, shapes, and colors available to evolve just the effect you've been imagining for your home.

And tile is not only for your floors and counter-tops. Try it on walls or even ceilings; trim doors and windows, fireplaces or mirrors; give your staircase a lift with decorated tile risers; add a special quality to the environment of your home with house numbers, super graphics, or even custom-designed tiles just for you. To see what we mean, take a stroll through the following pages and sample our smorgasbord of tile ideas; you're sure to come away with a few ideas of your own.

Applied to earth-toned quarry tiles, *hand-rubbed stain and plastic sealer create a warm elegance that enhances this home's eclectic interior. The stairs are trimmed in oak and coated with the same finish as the tile. Architect: George Cody.*

Quarry Tile: Simple and Elegant

Quarry tile—large, uniform, and devoid of decoration—is the most likely way to floor an entire home in ceramic tile. Usually available in earth tones, quarry tiles range from a raw, earthy Mexican appearance to the smartly sophisticated look of French glazed tiles. The four examples given here will show you the versatility of this material and the various forms in which it is available to you.

Most quarry tile is easy to maintain. For glazed types, damp-mopping is sufficient; unglazed quarry keeps its looks if treated with a sealer and then waxed periodically.

The Look of Leather, the Permanence of Tile
Used throughout the house, glazed 12" by 12" terra cotta quarry tile has a leatherlike appearance because of its rounded corners and edges and slightly uneven surface. Offsetting each row of tile adds visual interest. Architect: Fred Blecksmith.

Paver Tiles Add Punch
Distinguished by a rich brown patina from years of waxing and use, 6" by 10" machine-made clay paver tiles have an interesting surface of grooves and ridges formed as each tile was extruded. Architect: A. Quincy Jones.

Tiles for a Mexican Mood

Glazed 12″ by 12″ Mexican quarry tiles set with wide bands of white grout are effective as a flooring material throughout this Spanish-style home. Glazed quarry tiles are durable and easy to clean. Window trim of hand-decorated and glazed 4″ by 4″ Mexican tiles was set into wall before plastering, so wall face is flush with tiles. Architect: Alfred T. Gilman. Design: Windom Hawkins.

A Cultural Mix

An elegant, eclectic decor contrasts effectively with the simple boldness of Mexican quarry underfoot. These 11″ by 11″ unglazed terra cotta tiles keep their rustic but well-bred appearance with application of a sealer and periodic waxing. Architect: Stuart Baesel.

A Commercial Potpourri

Glazed commercial tiles might be considered commonplace; but one look at this collection of beautiful floors should counteract that impression. Though commercial tiles are uniform in appearance and widely available, applying them tastefully and inventively in suitable surroundings almost guarantees impressive results.

Manufacturers often provide a single type of tile in a wide range of colors, allowing you to select a small group of colors for a graphic design or a monochromatic theme. Unusual shapes such as hexagons, octagons, or even floral motifs will add visual interest to your floors. Or you can achieve a special look by using tile *seconds*. Usually sold at a low price, seconds can be put to excellent use, for any defects are usually quirks in appearance rather than deformities in the tiles themselves.

Tile Seconds: Impressive, Economical
At least five different shades of blue in random mix fuse visually to form this floor of 2″ square ceramic tiles. Leftovers from larger orders and pieces with slight irregularities, these tiles were purchased as seconds at a little more than half the normal retail price. The somewhat scattered color positioning blends tiles handsomely. Architect: Thaddeus E. Kusmierski.

Bold Design with a Quartet of Colors
Bright paths of ceramic tile direct the traffic in this modern home. Laid side by side on a mastic base, these 3″ by 6″ rectangular tiles create a bold impression. Architects: Ellmore/Titus.

A Scattering of Blooms

Recurring costs for floor refinishing induced the owners of this older Mexican-style home to tile the whole main floor with shaped ceramic paver tiles. Extruded into flat sheets and cut with cookie-cutter-like tools, three shapes create an interlocking floral pattern when laid with thin-set over the flat surface of the existing wood floor. Occasional paste waxing adds shine, protects tile surface. Design: The Tile Shop, Berkeley.

Framing Your Tile

As an alternative to an all-wood or all-tile floor, 8″ hexagonal ceramic tiles lie within prelaid strips of oak flooring. Though each material complements the other, placement of strips and tile requires careful planning. Architects: Churchill-Zlatunich Associates.

Effective Tile Accents

Here's a collection of inventive tile applications that use everything from commercial tiles to one-of-a-kind handmade and hand-decorated tiles. Often only a small amount of tile is required for an attractive and functional project, but sometimes a truly impressive effect can be achieved through use of a large expanse of tile in an unusual location, such as the firewall or ceiling on page 11.

· Most of these installations are ones you could take on yourself; some could be accomplished in a weekend. If you choose to do the tables, you may need a few additional skills—such as a knowledge of carpentry—to complete the project.

Serviceable Sideboard
Antique wall brackets support this simple but elegant dining room buffet. Although rectangular 2″ by 8″ tiles set in herringbone fashion require some cutting for proper fit, installation is relatively easy and inexpensive.

Tile Tables for Two
Four richly glazed tiles were made to order for each of these handmade cocktail tables. Since tiles are set in mastic without grout joints, this is a good one-day tile project. Floor is ceramic tile. Design: Ellis L. Jacobs.

Tile Risers Brighten Stairs
Work wonders in a weekend with just a few well-placed tiles. These stair risers, though decorated with custom painted and glazed 4″ by 6″ tiles, could as easily be done with commercially available designs. Design: Barbara Vantrease Beall Studio.

Dancing on the Ceiling

Ceiling panels of custom painted and glazed 6" by 6" tiles enliven an interior of dark wood and white walls. The tiles in each panel were anchored in thin-set adhesive row by row from a ladder-and-plank platform. Architect: Edward Carson Beall. Design: Barbara Vantrease Beall Studio.

Textures of Brick and Bark

Freestanding fireplace sits on stage of 6" by 9" unglazed plain tiles surrounded by companion relief tiles on back wall. Offset placement of ungrouted tiles gives a cobblestone appearance to this installation. Notice that bare tile edges need not always be covered with an extra trim. Architects: Ellmore/Titus.

Custom Stoneware

Handcut, painted, and glazed, these unusual 4" by 6" stoneware tiles were created by the artist specifically for this bathroom installation. Subdued earth tones of the glaze are reinforced by the use of stone gray grout. Architect: Bernard Judge. Design: Dora de Larios.

Tile Entryways . . . for a Warm Welcome

Home entryways really do have a special function: they say "welcome" to the outside world and give the visitor a glimpse of what awaits within. The tiled versions shown on these two pages have vastly different personalities, yet all invite the viewer to become further involved in each home.

The idea of a decorative tile entry can be pared down to simple eloquence, as in the entry below, or developed into an exciting mosaic swirl of color to charge up the visitor's senses (see photo on page 13, lower right). The ethnic ruglike entry at left hints at a traditional solution, while a field of black diamonds defines and divides the floor space of the home shown on page 13, upper left. All solutions are different, yet all are highly successful.

Ethnic Mix of Custom and Commercial Tiles
Hand-decorated, glazed tile entry simulates ethnic rug design of American Indian or African origin. Unglazed 4" by 6" tiles separating rows of glazed repeat designs make this an economical decorating idea. Design: Linda Rowlands with Barbara Vantrease Beall Studio.

Glazed Tile Entry Strip
Wide band of 12" by 12" glazed quarry tile set three tiles deep is flush with exterior entry and interior floor, effectively dividing these areas. Architects: Buff and Hensman, Architects and Associates.

Diamonds Define the Entry

Mock slate texture of cast clay tile, combined with effect of black tile insets in field of octagonal tiles, sets this entry area apart from the rest of a fully tiled interior. Diagonal set of white tiles in background adds subtle visual interest to an open expanse of floor. Architect: Peter Choate.

Mosaics Make Magic

Swirls of 2″ tile, meticulously cut and laid with mastic by a seasoned professional, form this fluid mosaic entry. Curved floor pattern contrasts with diagonal wood design of wall. Design: Charles J. Grebmeier.

Tile in the Kitchen

Here's a quintet of ideas for using tile in the kitchen. On this page, two kitchens take opposite approaches. Below, rectangular tiles in three shades of blue form bold patterns against regular arrays of the same tile; at left, glazed quarry tile and patterned resilient tile echo each other in a subtle harmony of earth tones.

The three photos opposite feature creative tile details: a durable *trompe l'oeil* rug, a tile border set in plaster, and a kitchen backsplash tiled with hardwood slices. Other kitchen ideas are shown on pages 16 and 17.

Dark Drama
Kitchen achieves an earthy elegance through a creative combination of ceramic and resilient tile. Rich brown glazed quarry tile is used on all work surfaces; on the floor, vinyl tile in similar but lighter tones adds subtle pattern interest. Color coordination is the key to the unified look. Design: Color Tile Supermart, Inc.

Elegant Egyptian Environment
Creamy white 10″ square floor tiles, textured in quarter-circle motifs, accentuate cool blues of counter tops and island mural. Ordinary 2″ by 6″ and 2″ by 8″ rectangular tiles, set in simple repeat pattern, create streamlined Egyptian look for contemporary kitchen. Design: Ray and Jackie Rossi, Designed Environ, Inc.

A Permanent Persian

One way to avoid cleaning bills: design and install a handpainted and glazed Persian rug. Or create your own area rug with decorated commercial tiles, then trim it with custom-painted and glazed fringe. Surrounding area is finished inexpensively with plain commercial tile. Design: Barbara Vantrease Beall Studio.

Old Tiles, New Statement

In remodeled historic adobe home, handpainted Mexican tiles stand out cheerfully around uncurtained window. Set directly in damp plaster, these tiles could also create the same effect if set and patched into chipped out areas of existing plaster. Architect: Will Shaw.

Wood Tiles Work Wonders

Unique 4" by 4" Uruguayan hardwood end-grain tiles form dramatic backsplash display. Fastened directly to wall without grout, in the sequence they were cut, these textural tiles complement the 3" cobalt blue ceramic tile counter top with wooden edging. Design: Al Garvey.

A Handpainted Botanical Design

Wall area behind cooktop is a natural for creative decor; this custom handpainted and glazed botanical design proves the point. The design relates both to the canisters at right and to a subtle but effective handpainted and glazed counter trim design. Design: Barbara Vantrease Beall Studio.

Tile Shelving

Kitchen shelf storage gets a pick-me-up with plain 4" by 4" white glazed commercial tiles. Easy to clean, these shelves are finished with sink cap tiles, a raised and rounded edging that keeps stored items from rolling off a shelf. Design: Barbara Vantrease Beall Studio.

Rustic Repeats Give Counter the Edge

Another way to edge a counter: a 90° angle formed with 4" by 4" and 2" by 4" hand-decorated Mexican tiles. White grout unifies the surface, giving the limelight to the tile decoration itself. Architect: Alfred T. Gilman. Design: Windom Hawkins.

Kitchen Tile Highlights

You needn't spread tile throughout your kitchen to achieve a delightfully detailed look. A few tile designs judiciously selected and applied will give a real uplift to an otherwise functional work area.

Counter tops and walls are the likeliest candidates for change, but to give your kitchen a real custom look, consider working with defined spaces such as the areas behind the cooktop or the kickplates below the lower cabinets. If you're interested in ceramics, you might even design and execute your own decorative tiles for a truly personalized kitchen.

French Glass Tiles . . . for a Colorful Accent
Elegant 1″ French glass hexagonal tiles shown here are available in a variety of patterns. Installation is a simple task, as tiles come mounted on 12″ square mesh-backed sheets. Design: International Tile and Supply Corp. Kitchen Design: Matt Wolf, Kitchens Etcetera.

Kickplate of Culinarios Tiles

Instead of a wood or metal kickplate, try trimming your kitchen floor with culinarios tiles instead. Though the tiles shown here were custom handpainted and glazed, other versions are readily available commercially. Design: Barbara Vantrease Beall Studio.

Design on the Diagonal
Embossed resilient tiles positioned on the diagonal add a strong regional flair to cozy den spiced with American Indian accents. By avoiding conventional installation, the designer has not only emphasized the strength of the tile design but also visually enlarged a basically small room. Design: Armstrong Cork Company.

Smooth as Slate
Classic mood of this bedroom/sitting room owes much of its elegance to a carefully selected floor covering of white, slate-textured resilient tiles. Offsetting tile squares in a checker-board arrangement develops interesting patterns of light and shadow on this flooring.

Brick on a Budget
Strong offset brick pattern of resilient tiles blends with hand-painted and glazed culinarios counter top ceramic tiles to emphasize the country look of this cheerful kitchen. Easy on the feet and the back, resilient tile is a good choice for kitchen work areas. Kitchen Design: Diane Johnson. Counter top tile design: Barbara Vantrease Beall Studio.

Wood and Resilient Tiles . . . Attractive Alternatives

Resilient and parquet tiles are two extremely versatile alternatives to ceramic tile. As with ceramics, both come in standard sizes and shapes that are easy to apply. The examples here merely give a sampling of the many patterns available in each type of product.

Resilient tiles can pretend to any number of personalities, from brick to slate or even ceramic. Parquet, on the other hand, has a distinct identity of its own. An aura of permanence and old-world quality surrounds this wood product, for it adds a feeling of well-bred style to practically any environment.

Wood Tiles of Teak
Teak parquet floor in Haddon Hall pattern consists of 12" squares of solid wood strips glued together on mesh backing. Edges are bevelled slightly so that each tile is distinguishable. This type of wooden tile is easily installed on floor with mastic. Table is covered with wood tiles. Architects: Ellmore/Titus.

The Warmth of Wood
Unusual oak parquet kitchen counter consists of 6" square tiles set perpendicular to one another in mastic, then framed in oak trim and varnished for protection. Each tile consists of seven 7/8" by 6" solid strips of wood held together by metal splines. Design: Charles Bliss.

Being Expansive with Parquet
Placing fingered parquet tiles in parallel rows, rather than in a checkerboard pattern as in the photograph at left, creates an entirely different feeling that visually expands this living area. Architect: John Brooks Boyd.

Creative Baths with Commercial Tile

Inventive yet tasteful, the 10 tile installations on the following four pages all use commercial ceramic tile to complete the promise of a well-designed bath environment. Decorative touches in each bath design make use of inherent characteristics of tile; plant niches, curved surfaces, supergraphics, contrasting colors, and other design ideas give each bath a distinct personality based on the standard, repeatable appearance of commercial tiles.

Getting the Angle on a Great Graphic
Plain 4″ by 4″ commercial tiles can make strong graphic statements; cutting some tiles diagonally enabled the architect to build an expansive wraparound design for this soaking tub and shower enclosure. Architect: Gary Gilbar.

Clean-Cut European
Two colors of 1″ square tesserae tile define both form and function in a modern Italian-style bath. Bright red floor grouted in white joins the main bath to an open shower in rear, optically expanding the appearance of what is essentially a standard-size bathroom. Tiles come in 12″ by 12″ mesh-back sheets. Architect: David Raphael Singer.

Shower in the Great Outdoors

Secluded, woodsy setting inspired inclusion of dramatic window in this sunken tub and shower. Simply elegant, these 3" by 6" green tiles, glazed to a glossy shine, are custom-set in a prepared mortar bed. Architects: Ellmore/Titus.

Brown and White Cross Paths

Effective and efficient use of a limited number of decorative custom tiles adds variety to this predominantly commercial tile bath at minimum cost. Though a vast amount of work is involved here, an ardent and adept do-it-yourselfer could probably take on a similar job. The work of mortaring and tiling the tub is avoided by use of a standard tub. A job like this is not a weekend affair—be sure to plan every step carefully ahead of time.

A Soaking Tub . . . Tile Inside and Out

Less expensive than outfitting this large area in hand-decorated tile, using a single design of handpainted Italian tile as trim for plain rectangular tiles defines design of an Egyptian-style custom bath. Design: Ray and Jackie Rossi, Designed Environ, Inc.

Two-Tone Treasure
Giant tub built in mortar base is like a small child's swimming pool; wide ledges fore and aft hold a collection of houseplants. Blue 3″ by 6″ rectangular floor tiles pick up flecks of blue in neutral-toned 2″ square tub tiles. Architect: Martin Garfinkel.

Scenic Trim Goes Traditional
A large expanse of decoration isn't necessary to make a tile environment come alive; this tastefully restrained bath with shower features a narrow band of handpainted and glazed 4″ by 6″ tiles in a running hunt scene. Decorated outer base trim banding and diagonally set shower floor unify the decor, which is completed with plain 4″ by 6″ commercial tiles. Design: Barbara Vantrease Beall Studio.

A Sculptured Environment
Plaster, wood, glass, and tile create an expansive custom-built bath environment. Sunken tile tub takes advantage of a city view, while three-dimensional, amorphous plaster walls finish off previously laid tile areas above counter top. Architect: Igor Sazevich.

Plants Find Their Niche
Modern in mood, this step-in tile shower of 12″ by 12″ glazed quarry tiles has built-in 6″ by 11″ square plant niches of same tile to take advantage of the skylight and the moist environment. Architects: Buff and Hensman, Architects and Associates.

Tile in the Round
A study in applying a flat medium to curved surfaces, this custom shower/bath environment approaches sculptural art. Curvilinear design of shower alcove at left and sunken Japanese soaking tub was worked in plain 1″ by 3″ tiles. Architects: Ellmore/Titus.

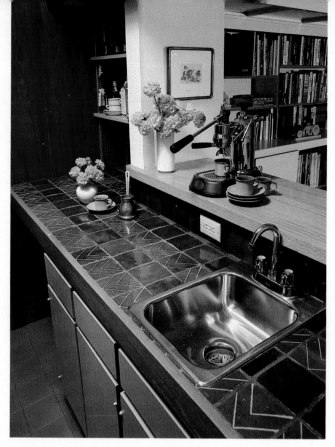

Tile Finishes with Flair

Sometimes the little details are what make a tile job stand out. These five examples show how the inherent qualities of a tile type can be enhanced by special finishing treatments.

One needn't settle for a conventional method of installing or completing a tile job; in fact, the more creative you are in dealing with a common situation, the more personalized your finished installation will appear. Though two of the methods shown here—the quarter-round and the mitered edging—are jobs for experienced tile setters if not professionals, the other methods are within the reach of most do-it-yourselfers.

Wet Bar . . . Simple but Effective
A built-in wet bar takes on an updated look through application of chocolate-colored scraffito decorated 6" by 6" Mexican tiles. This would be easy for the homeowner who wants a weekend job with maximum impact. Note wood counter edge. Architect: Bernard Judge.

Vanity of Penny-round Tiles
Curved edges of this counter and backsplash are built of mortar, then "draped" in penny-round tiles mounted on mesh-backed sheets. Design is simple but could prove difficult to install—plan carefully for satisfactory results. Architect: Thaddeus E. Kusmierski.

South of the Border Style

Enhanced by use of hand-decorated and glazed Mexican tiles, bullnose tile pieces are a traditional method for edging a ceramic counter top. Vine pattern on 4″ by 4″ and 2″ by 4″ tile trim ties in with basin and backsplash. Architect: Alfred T. Gilman. Design: Windom Hawkins.

Quarter-Round Trim Treatment

Narrow quarter-round tile pieces set in mortar base offer an attractive alternative treatment for bathroom basin trim. Cutting tiles to fit and floating them into mortar are both difficult and time-consuming tasks. Design: Tile by Buzz.

Bevel-Edged Beauty

Standard tile trims don't always come in colors or sizes you need. An attractive solution, this custom bevelled-edge counter uses 1″ tiles set at angles in a mortar base as an effective finishing trim. Architect: Wayne Wedell. Design: Richard and Linda Diamond.

The Total Tile Bath

Bathrooms have a special place in the hearts of many who consider water as one of the elemental joys of life. These connoisseurs find nothing too good for the space in which they perform their daily toilette. Witness the four unique offerings served up on these two pages.

These imaginative baths give esthetic answers to practical questions. The tiles range from costly custom patterns to handsome yet budget-minded products available coast-to-coast. In each case, though, their function is the same: to provide durable beauty in a room that too often is simply utilitarian.

A Charming Chameleon
A process called fuming produced the unusual iridescent quality of these 11″ by 11″ glazed Italian tiles. The appearance of the tile alters from pink to gold to blue as light passes across the tub enclosure. French glass 1″ hexagons on mesh backing form the curved backrest and floor of the tub. Design: Tom McGraw with International Tile and Supply Corporation.

The Greenhouse Goes Indoors
Bath environment of ferns and vines integrates tub enclosure and shelf/seating area. Handpainted and glazed 6″ by 6″ tiles were first numbered on backs according to a graphed layout plan, then installed over a waterproofed lath-and-cement tub surround. Design: Barbara Vantrease Beall Studio.

Beauty through Simplicity

Two widely available commercial tile patterns combine in this adaptable bathroom design. One pattern is used on the walls, the other primarily on the floor. An accent band of the floor tile adds a dramatic touch to the walls, greatly enhancing the overall scheme. Design: Color Tile Supermart, Inc.

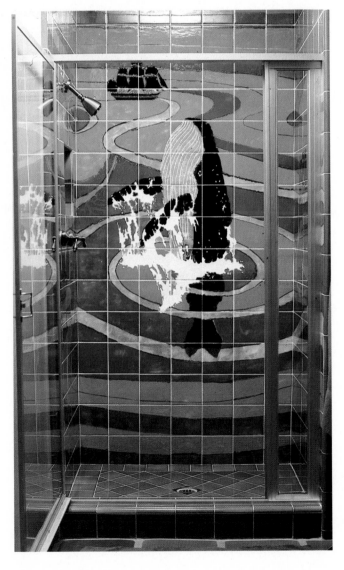

Shower Ahoy!

Impressive hand-decorated and glazed tiles of this shower wall form the focal point of a nautically decorated boy's bath. Though tiling a shower enclosure may require a pro, the effect obtained can be extraordinary. Note the diagonal pattern of plain tiles on the shower floor. Design: Barbara Vantrease Beall Studio.

Tile Complements the Hearth

At the heart of many homes is the fireplace. Originally intended as functional heating devices, fireplaces have developed over the years into decorative focal points as well. Here are four different versions using tile— each with its own brand of function and style.

Tile is an ideal material for fireplace use as an alternative to the usual brick, cement, or metal enclosure. Impervious to heat and easy to clean because of its glossy surface, ceramic tile also provides a medium for artistic expression. Though custom-designed tiles have been used in three of the four installations shown here, well-designed commercial tiles could do the job with great success.

Entertaining Idea in the Round
Handmade and hand-decorated to owner's specifications, trapezoidal tiles in a sunburst pattern of concentric circles dramatize a contemporary firepit. Tile work could be done by homeowner after hearth base is constructed to meet building codes.

California-style Floral Fireplace
Hand-decorated and glazed tiles feature bright flowers bordered and trimmed by bands of yellow. After 6" by 6" tiles were set around the face of the fireplace, plaster of surrounding wall was gradually built up flush with the tile. Design: Barbara Vantrease Beall Studio.

Greenery Garlands Frame a Flame
Lush with magnolia blossoms, these hand-decorated and glazed tiles join with a handsome wood mantel to update an old brick fireplace. Installation was fairly simple— tiles were applied to existing bricks with mastic. Had brick surface been uneven, however, a mortar base would have been necessary. Design: Susan Tait, The Tile Shop, Berkeley.

Deft Delft: Collector's Pride and Joy
Traditionally styled, this brick and tile fireplace effectively displays a collection of fine antique Delft tiles. The same effect could be achieved with modern 6″ by 6″ Delft tiles. Architect: Alfred T. Gilman. Design: Windom Hawkins.

Letter-Perfect Mailboxes

A neighborhood project for experienced do-it-yourselfers: grouped mailboxes with a custom handpainted and glazed ceramic plaque for each box. Stone and concrete structure was built around boxes, which were then faced with plaques and wood trim. Design: Barbara Vantrease Beall Studio.

Taking Tile Out-of-Doors

Though tiles have appeared predominantly in interior settings on the previous pages, don't forget that their attractive permanence makes them ideal for outdoor use as well. These four interesting ideas add a level of quality and taste to otherwise mundane, functional situations.

Murals and trims are simple additions to exterior environments; these installations are well within the scope of a weekend do-it-yourself project. The mailboxes and entry steps require more planning and construction time; but the results would enhance the exterior of any home.

Tile Plaques in the Mayan Manner

Limited front yard space spurred owners to substitute this decorative wood and tile wall for established plantings. The hand-decorated and glazed 6" by 6" tiles were first mounted without grout on wood panels, then set into fence. Design: Joan Fey with Barbara Vantrease Beall Studio.

Tiles over Concrete

Sand-colored tiles, patterned after the floor Jefferson created for Monticello, transform cold concrete slabs into a more congenial entry. Existing slab is decorated by individual hexagonal and square tiles laid on mastic base to form large overall octagonal pattern. You can complete each block individually before moving on to the next one. Design: Ray and Jackie Rossi, Designed Environ, Inc.

Tile Trim's Warm Welcome

Handpainted and glazed 4″ by 4″ tiles with circular motifs edge a wood-trimmed entryway. Wall was prepared by attaching a 2″ by 4″ wooden backing along edge of door; tiles were then applied to backing with thin-set adhesive. A 2″-wide metal strip conceals the raw edges of wood and tile. Design: Barbara Vantrease Beall Studio.

CERAMIC TILE
. . . a colorful, lasting surface

Molded plastic spacers *help the tilesetter to correctly lay and space glazed quarry tiles in mastic on a plywood subfloor. The spacers can be either covered with grout and left in place, or pried up and removed when mastic sets.*

Whether you're building a new home or remodeling an older one, you'll find few surfacing materials that can match the decorative impact, versatility, and permanence of ceramic tile.

Basically a slab of hard-baked clay, ceramic tile provides a surface that's fireproof, durable, mar-resistant, impervious to soil and moisture, and easy to maintain. A tiled surface consists of a series or group of tiles, each fastened with an adhesive (also known as a bonding agent or a bond coat) to a subsurface or "backing" and usually bonded to its neighbors with a filler material called grout.

Ceramic tile comes in a seemingly endless variety of colors, patterns, and surface textures. Besides its many esthetic and functional advantages, ceramic tile will add value to your home.

When you use ceramic tile, you're using a proven product. It is one of the oldest, most successful surfacing materials: tiles have been found in structures of the ancient Egyptian and Roman cultures. Brilliantly colored ceramic tiles still beautify the floors, walls, and ceilings of cathedrals, temples, and palaces built many hundreds of years ago.

Where to Use Ceramic Tile

At one time, the use of ceramic tile in the home was restricted to the bathroom and an occasional entry foyer. Around the turn of the century, however, ceramic tile became popular for use in almost any room in the house. Today, ceramic tile may be found in many areas: on floors, walls, storage shelves, and kitchen counters and backsplashes; as table tops; around tubs and showers; and even on ceilings. In addition, some ceramic tiles are suitable for use as garden and patio paving.

Floors. Ceramic tile is a natural for floors. Nothing tolerates foot traffic as well as tile. In entryways, halls, and other heavy-traffic corridors, ceramic floor tiles remain rigid and colorfast. An onslaught of wet galoshes or the innocent tracking of a muddy family pet will do no harm to the floor. In the kitchen or bathroom, ceramic tile provides excellent protection against drips and spills; cleaning requires only a damp sponge or cloth.

Visually, a tiled floor can add a strong decorative accent. Depending on the tile, you can create any atmosphere from elegance to rustic informality. Brighten a dark room with a tile floor, or make a room look larger by extending the tile floor onto the patio or deck.

Walls. Any wall that might receive spray or a splash is an obvious candidate for ceramic tile. Around bathtubs and showers, tile provides a waterproof surface that is easy to keep clean of water spots and soap film. And you needn't limit tile to walls that get wet. A wall of ceramic tile in a living room, dining room, or den adds a dramatic backdrop for furnishings, plants, or a freestanding fireplace.

Counter tops. Ideal as a working surface around the kitchen sink and stove top, ceramic tile is equally unaffected by a sharp knife edge or a hot pan. Grease and food spots wipe off easily. Tile also adds a functional, decorative surface to a bathroom vanity, an eating counter, or a wet bar. Adding a new ceramic tile top will give new life to an old table; tile also adds flair to exposed storage shelves.

Fireplaces. Because they are baked at high temperatures, ceramic tiles are not affected by heat and are thus appropriate for use on a fireplace hearth or facing. Line the inside perimeter of the fireplace, or outline the outside face; even a single row of tile will give an old fireplace a new look.

Stairs and steps. Frequent up and down traffic seems to take a special toll on the treads of stairs and steps. Ceramic tiles with a slip-resistant surface may be the answer. Bright-colored tiles set against the risers of the steps add an interesting decorative touch as well as making the steps more distinct—an especially helpful feature along dark halls or staircases.

Decorative borders. Set edge-to-edge or spaced apart, tiles make a beautiful border to accent a door or window, a wall or ceiling fixture, or an entire room. If fastened to the surface and left raised, they may require wood or metal border trim. As a border around a door or window, tiles can be set into the plaster or stucco, so that tile faces are flush with the finished wall.

Outdoors. Many kinds of ceramic tiles are suitable for outdoor use as a paving material or decorative surfacing. Extending the tile floor of a room out onto an adjoining deck or patio creates a strong visual tie, making both areas appear larger. A garden pool or swimming pool lined or rimmed with ceramic tile adds an elegant accent to the garden. A tile fountain can add a colorful highlight and brighten a dark corner of the yard.

Some Facts about Ceramic Tile

Once you've decided to use ceramic tile, another choice still confronts you: what kind should you get? Before you tackle this one, stop and find out something about ceramic tile—types, characteristics, colors, shapes, and uses.

When you shop for ceramic tile, you'll find that tile is either glazed or unglazed.

Glazed tile. If the color of the tile was applied to the surface of the clay body (known as the bisque) before final baking, the tile is glazed. Glazes can have several finishes: high gloss; a satinlike matte finish; semimatte; or a dull, pebbly-textured finish.

Unglazed tile. The color in these tiles runs throughout the body—either the natural clay colors or pigments mixed with the clay prior to forming and baking.

Tile bodies are rated according to how easily they absorb water. Porcelain is the most vitreous (glasslike), least water-absorbent tile body. Common glazed wall tiles have the least vitreous, most water-absorbent body. (The tile is made water resistant by the glazing on the surface.)

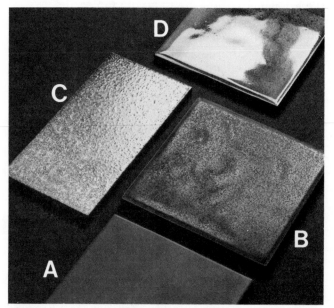

Finishes *on ceramic tiles vary from dull unglazed surfaces to shiny glazed ones. Shown here: unglazed (A), matte (B), semi-matte (C), and bright glossy finish (D).*

Generally, ceramic tiles are made in three basic forms: wall tiles, floor tiles, and ceramic mosaics.

Floor Tiles

Available unglazed or glazed, so-called floor tiles are generally larger and thicker than wall tiles. Their superior strength makes them more durable underfoot. Floor tiles come as squares, rectangles, hexagons, and octagons as well as in Moorish, ogee, and other exotic shapes (see next page).

Unglazed tile has advantages for floor use: it is less slippery, and wear does not show because the coloration extends throughout the body. Glazed floor tiles have textured, matte surfaces to give better traction and longer wear.

Floor tiles are of four general kinds: quarry tiles, pavers, patio, and glazed. (For installation pointers, see page 48.)

Quarry tiles. These tiles commonly come unglazed, in natural clay colors, but they are available with colorful glazed surfaces as well. Thicknesses range from ⅜" to ½", with surfaces from 6" by 6" and 4" by 8" to 12" by 12". Rough and water-resistant, quarry tile is an ideal flooring surface both indoors and out. Quarry tile also offers a variety of trim pieces.

Pavers. Like most quarry tiles, pavers are unglazed and water-resistant. These rugged tiles, available in many colors, come in three standard sizes: 4" by 4" by ⅜", 6" by 6" by ½", and 4" by 8" by ½".

Patio tiles. Mostly nonvitreous (absorbing water easily) patio tiles are thicker and less regular in shape than quarry tiles or pavers. Up to 1" in thickness and 12" by 12" in size, patio tiles have a rough appearance reminiscent of the handmade tiles put down by early settlers. Colors are reds, tans, and browns. They may shatter if frozen.

Glazed tiles. Imported glazed floor tiles, plain and decorated, usually 8" by 8", are becoming increasingly popular. Many of these are finished with matte and textured surfaces to reduce the chance of slipping.

Wall Tiles

Tiles classified as wall tiles are glazed and offer a great variety of colors and designs. Generally lighter and thinner than floor tiles, wall tiles are appropriate primarily for use on interior surfaces: walls, counter tops, and ceilings. Their bodies are fairly light—a plus for vertical installation. And though the bodies are porous, the glazing process makes the surface water-resistant. Wall tiles can be used on interior floors if traffic is light.

Standard sizes for wall tiles range from 3" by 3" to 4¼" by 8½", with thicknesses from ¼" to ⅜". As a visit to a dealer will show you, other sizes and shapes are available.

Many tiles come with matching trim pieces. Carrying such intriguing names as "bullnose cap,"

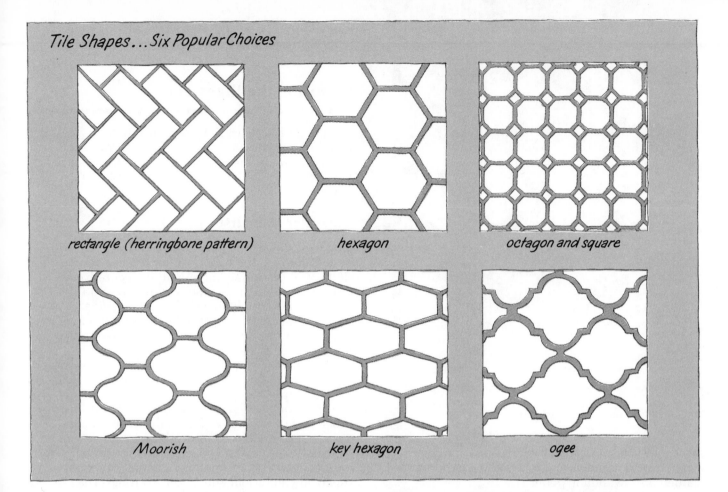

Tile Shapes...Six Popular Choices

rectangle (herringbone pattern)

hexagon

octagon and square

Moorish

key hexagon

ogee

"eagle beak," and "up butterfly," these specially shaped pieces are designed to finish off edges, form coves, and turn inside and outside corners (see illustrations at right). Some tiles have matching glazed ceramic accessories such as soap dishes, towel bars, and glass and brush holders.

Some wall tiles have small ceramic spacers molded onto their edges to keep spacing equal as tiles are laid. Butted together, the spacers maintain uniform joint spacing for grout throughout the surface. (For installation pointers, see page 51.)

Panels. Wall tiles are now available in the form of pregrouted panels. Designed primarily for shower and tub areas, the panels contain up to sixty-four 4¼" by 4¼" tiles each. The savings in installation time are considerable. The panels are grouted with a flexible, water-repellent silicone, urethane, or polyvinyl chloride rubber.

Ceramic Mosaics

Tiles sold under this name are generally small—up to 2" by 2" in size. They come in groups, either mounted on a thread mesh or paper backing or joined with silicone rubber.

Ceramic mosaic is among the most colorful and versatile materials in the tile family. Not only is it

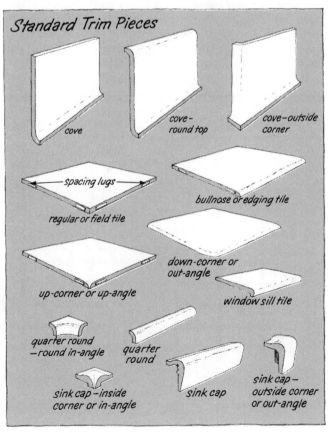

Standard Trim Pieces

cove

cove–round top

cove–outside corner

spacing lugs

regular or field tile

bullnose or edging tile

up-corner or up-angle

down-corner or out-angle

window sill tile

quarter round –round in-angle

quarter round

sink cap–inside corner or in-angle

sink cap

sink cap– outside corner or out-angle

CERAMIC TILE **35**

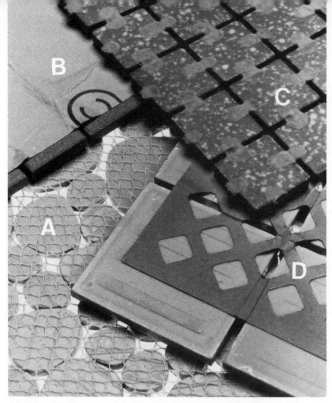

Mosaic tiles *come mounted on thread mesh (A), paper sheet (B), silicone rubber (C), and paper mesh (D). You may find tiles up to 6″ square mounted in sheets.*

handsome on smooth floors and walls, but it can wrap around columns and follow the contours of garden and swimming pools.

Mosaics can be of natural clay tile or hard porcelain. Traditionally mosaic tile was unglazed; instead, color pigments were added to the body material, coloring the tile throughout. In addition to traditional mosaic tile, you will find many glazed, patterned varieties measuring up to 3″ across and available in teardrop and other nontraditional shapes. All are mesh-mounted for easier installation.

Baked at higher temperatures than most other tiles, porcelain mosaic tiles have a harder, denser body; both glazed and unglazed varieties are impervious to water.

Choosing the Right Tile

Installing ceramic tile can be a sizable financial commitment; the permanence of tile is not compatible with a change of mind. As a result, choosing the right tile to fill your functional and decorative needs is crucial.

Consider Use First

How you will use the tile surface and where it will be installed are the two most important considerations. Will the surface be primarily decorative, or must it stand up under a steady stream of traffic? Do you want it to brighten a dark room or add a subdued rustic mood to a light study? If the family bathroom is the site, you'll have a different set of requirements than you would for the entry hall.

You have a lot to think about when considering your use of the tile, and you may want some help. Here are three ready sources:

Showrooms. Ceramic tile manufacturers, distributors, and dealers, as well as some licensed contractors, have showrooms displaying a great variety of tiles. Not only can you examine the tile, but you can see its use in a sampling of actual situations—especially bathroom and kitchen settings. The showroom staff will gladly answer your questions and advise you on tile selections, amounts, and costs. In addition you may find a collection of catalogs featuring additional tile varieties that can be ordered specially.

These showrooms and the literature they offer can be an important source for ideas on types, colors, and possible patterns. Here, too, you can get the names of tile contractors should you decide not to tackle the installation job yourself.

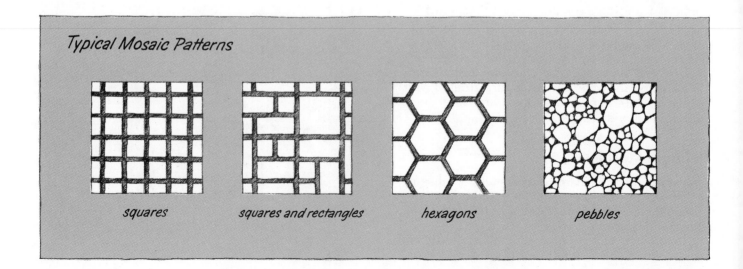

Typical Mosaic Patterns

squares   squares and rectangles   hexagons   pebbles

Decorators or architects. These professionals specialize in combining esthetics and function. They can help you analyze your needs and find solutions to tricky decorating problems.

Tile contractors. For help on installation, answers to structural questions, and guidance on tile selection, a tile contractor can be a valuable source.

Most tile contractors will show you a few samples of tiles, help you with basic choices, and estimate quantities, prices, and labor costs for the installation.

Think about the Foundation

Tile, like a house, is only as strong as its foundation. The surface over which the ceramic tile will be installed—known as the backing (see page 42)—is an important consideration when you choose tile. The composition and structural soundness of this surface will not only limit the kinds of tile you can lay over it, it will determine the quality and durability of the finished tile surface. Here are the most

Seeing colors *and patterns of tiles and sample installations in a showroom can help you make a choice.*

Tips on Designing with Tile

At one time or another, we've all been fooled by optical illusions— remember "Which line is longer?" and "Which square is larger?" You can put these same illusions to work for you when you use tile colors, patterns, and designs to alter or control the apparent space in a room. Here are a few tips:

A busy tile pattern or a mix of several colors will make an area look smaller; use of a simple pattern and a single color has the opposite effect.

Small tiles seem to expand the size of the tiled surface. Large tiles decrease the apparent size of the area.

Dark colors will tend to shrink a given space . . .

. . . while light or bright colors impart an airy, spacious feeling.

To achieve visual unity, continue the same flooring from one room to the next or out onto an exterior patio area.

Divide space within a room into specific activity areas by using contrasting tile colors or patterns on the floor.

Put tile to work: *Repeated tile pattern running lengthwise adds depth to room; running across, it gives a shorter, wider look. Tile continued outside increases apparent space, adds visual unity.*

common surfaces you might cover with ceramic tile:

Wood. This category includes plywood, tongue-and-groove subfloor, and existing wood floors (see pages 43 and 44).

Concrete slab. Either a newly poured slab floor or an existing one makes an excellent foundation for ceramic tile (see page 44).

Gypsum wallboard. For walls, this is the most common existing surface. Careful preparation is always a must; sometimes replacement may be necessary. For installation over gypsum wallboard, the lighter weight, glazed wall tiles are frequently favored (see pages 43 and 44).

Resilient floors. An existing solid and thoroughly clean resilient floor, either tiles or sheet material, can be covered with ceramic tiles. Heavier tiles, such as quarry tile, are a good choice over this kind of floor (see page 44).

Existing ceramic tile. You can cover an existing ceramic tile surface with a new layer of ceramic tile—*if* the old is still in good condition (see page 45).

When in doubt . . . get advice. If you're unsure about the soundness of the surface to be tiled, it's best to consult a professional. An experienced tile dealer or contractor can quickly assess what's needed, whether it's a simple cleaning of the old surface, repair and reinforcing, or a complete replacement of the backing.

Custom Tile and Glazing —Another Alternative

If catalog shopping and a showroom search has left you without a satisfactory tile, consider having a tile made to order. Customizing tile is done mostly in the glazing process. Custom tile manufacturers will glaze "raw" (unglazed) tiles to the color and pattern of your choice. Or, as a less expensive alternative, customize stock tile with specially-made decals.

Hand-painted custom glazing can create most any pattern you can imagine. A group of tiles can be decorated to look like an exotic rug permanently glazed into the floor surface; or a tiny corner piece can be accented with a delicate flower.

Special tile manufacturers can also create tile in odd shapes and sizes to fill specific custom design needs.

A Word about Cost

Tile can cost from about $1 per square foot to nearly $40. Generally, the more tiles of a particular size, surface pattern, and glaze that are manufactured, the less each one will cost you—a result of the efficiency of mass production. Special surface treatment, such as glazing and texturing, and manufacturing in smaller batches mean higher prices.

Single-color, glazed, flat-surfaced tiles—those commonly used around showers and tubs—are the most economical, sometimes less than $1 per square foot. The trim pieces for these tiles normally cost

more per square foot than the regular squares. Three-dimensional patterns and multicolored glazes can easily double those costs. Other cost factors include the purity and density of the clay used and the temperature at which the tiles are baked. Purer clays fired at higher temperatures generally make costlier but better wearing tiles.

Buying Tile

When you are ready to select and purchase your ceramic tile, the following tips may prove helpful:

Measure. Have accurate measurements ready for the area to be covered. A plan on graph paper helps you to visualize the area and provides a clue to the trim pieces you may need. Your tile dealer will help you figure out how many tiles you require.

Buy extra. Always buy a few more tiles than you need—usually 2 to 5 percent additional. Then you'll have an extra tile to replace one that's cut to the wrong size or damaged during installation. Also, should a tile chip or crack while in use, you'll have a matching tile to replace it with. If you wait until damage occurs to buy replacement tiles, you may not be able to find tile that matches: colors can vary from shipment to shipment, or the manufacturer may discontinue them.

Check for color. Before you bring the tiles home, check the cartons to be sure the shades of color on the tiles match. Different cartons of the same tile can vary slightly.

Watch for closeouts. A dealer will often sell "closeouts" at a discount. These may be tiles the manufacturer has discontinued, a color or pattern that was overstocked, or a supply of tiles left over from a large installation or a cancelled order.

Check the "bone pile." Another way to save money is to select tiles from the dealer's or manufacturer's bone pile. These tiles, called "seconds," are flawed or blemished (usually only slightly), so they cannot be sold with the regular stock at regular prices. Often these tiles will go undetected if randomly mixed with unblemished tile. Entire installations have been done with such "reject tiles" at great savings.

You Will also Need Adhesive and Grout

When you select and buy ceramic tile, also get the adhesive (to hold the tile to the backing) and the grout (the mortarlike material which fills the joints between the tiles).

If you choose to have the installation done professionally, then the tile contractor will know which adhesive and grout to use for the most satisfactory results. Many professionals prefer the traditional method of setting the tiles in a bed of mortar. But this method is tricky, especially indoors and on walls, and is probably not one to try on your own.

Adhesives: Making It Stick

Though most professional tile setters prefer the traditional mortar bed, other adhesives, developed in recent years, shorten installation time and simplify construction. These newer adhesives have proven a boon for do-it-yourself tile setters. Applied over a variety of backings, they enable amateurs to undertake tile projects that were formerly beyond their abilities.

Collectively, these adhesives are called thin-sets or thin-beds to differentiate them from the traditional thick mortar bed. They are applied about 3/32" thick. These thin-sets do not require a mortar bed backing, nor do tiles need to be soaked prior to installing—a necessity with the traditional method.

Thin-set adhesives are of three types: those with an organic base, those with a cement base, and those with an epoxy base. Which adhesive you choose depends on the type of tile and the kind of surface you want to put it on. Consult your dealer and carefully read the label on the adhesive container to make sure it will work in your situation.

Organic adhesives. Commonly known as mastics, these adhesives are the most popular with do-it-yourselfers. There are two main types; both come in paste form.

Type I, or water-resistant, mastics are formulated with a solvent. They are recommended for damp areas such as bathrooms and counter tops. Type I mastics are flammable and may irritate the skin and lungs, so keep fire away and ventilate the working area well.

Type II mastics are formulated with latex. They are less irritating to skin and easier to clean up. However, they should be used only in dry areas such as entryways, dining rooms, and family rooms.

Whether you buy Type I or Type II mastic, make sure it is designed for the use you intend—wall or floor. Mastic intended for walls dries more slowly and has a longer open time than mastic meant for floor use.

Suitable backings for mastics include smooth plaster, gypsum wallboard, plywood, masonry, wood, dry concrete, terrazzo, and plastic laminates. If you have a concrete floor with embedded radiant heating pipes, turn off the heat before application. Allow the mastic to cure for 24 hours. If using mastic to install tile on a fireplace, allow mastic to cure the same length of time.

Cement-based adhesives. These are commonly called mortars, are not flammable, and can be cleaned up with water. Both types, dry-set and latex–Portland cement mortars, must be mixed with sand before use; however, they can be purchased presanded.

• *Dry-set mortars* are the original thin-bed adhesives. The term "dry-set" indicates that the tiles are not soaked in water as they are for the traditional mortar bed method. Dry-sets are prepared by mixing with water according to directions on the package.

Adhesives and grouts *come in bewildering variety; consult your dealer for proper selection.*

• *Latex-Portland cement mortars* are similar to dry-sets but are mixed with liquid latex. Use the brand of dry mortar mix specified by the latex manufacturer. Directions on the package of dry mortar mix will give the proportion of latex required. Some brands of latex must be diluted with water. If you use this type, do the diluting before you mix with the dry mortar mix. This mortar is easier to use and more supple than dry-set, and it has greater water resistance.

Either mortar should be allowed to stand for 15 minutes after mixing; it should then be remixed before it is applied to the backing. The consistency should be such that the mortar ridges formed on the backing by the notched trowel do not slump or flow.

If a film forms on the applied mortar, stop laying tiles, scrape off the mortar, and apply fresh material.

Suitable backings include dry cement slabs, if completely free from paint or other coatings (see page 44), backer board, gypsum wallboard, ceramic tile, marble, and brick. Don't use wood, even if it has been primed or sealed—it may swell. And avoid vinyl, asphalt, and linoleum surfaces, too; cement adhesives don't adhere well to these synthetics.

Epoxy-based adhesives. For these, you must mix two or three accurately measured ingredients just prior to application. In addition, epoxies are more expensive than other adhesives.

• *Epoxy mortars* are useful where chemical resistance of floors and high bond and impact strengths are required.

• *Epoxy adhesives* have somewhat less chemical resistance than epoxy mortars but are easier to apply. Their tendency to ooze makes them easier to use on floors than on walls. They are good adhesives over plywood for counters and floors in wet areas.

Epoxies are tricky to use. Not only is their hardening time difficult to control, but they must be applied when the temperature is between 60° and 90°. They are also more difficult to clean off the tiles' surface when set. Be sure to wear rubber gloves—epoxy adhesives can cause skin poisoning.

Suitable backings for epoxy include dry cement slabs (including those with radiant heat), backer board, gypsum wallboard, wood (including wood covered with vinyl, asphalt, or linoleum), ceramic tile, marble, and brick.

Grouts: Cosmetic and Functional

Grouts are the materials that highlight the tile pattern and fill the joints between tiles, keeping out foreign matter such as dirt, food, and—if sealed—liquids. Even when tiles are laid on cement with cement mortars, water and other liquids penetrating behind the tiles can discolor them and destroy the adhesive bond and backing. Even small cracks in the grout can allow water to penetrate, so it is important to apply the grout correctly, and to protect and care for it properly (see care suggestions on page 63).

The three basic categories of grout are: cement-based grout, silicone rubber, and epoxy grout.

The grout you choose depends upon the tile type, location, joint width, and adhesive. Consult your tile dealer and check the label on the grout package. (See page 62 for additional information on grouts and how to apply them.)

A few tips. To hide irregularities in alignment of the tiles, use a grout whose color matches that of the tile. Use a dark grout on working surfaces, such as the kitchen counter, as it will not show stains. Before you apply a dark, contrasting grout, make sure it will not stain the surface of the tiles, especially unglazed tiles. Generally, try to match the grout to the dominant color of the tiles unless you are trying to add variety to an expansive tile surface.

Cement-based grouts. These are the most commonly used grouts by both amateur and professional tile setters. They consist of a base of Portland cement modified to provide such specific characteristics as water retention, hardness, flexibility, uniformity, and whiteness. When buying, examine the grout for freshness. If the grains of cement and sand tend to ball together, the grout is stale; choose a fresher batch.

• *Dry-set grouts* are similar to the dry-set mortars (see page 39). They can be used to grout both wall and floor tiles. You can buy these grouts premixed with additives: just mix in water when ready for use. The grout manufacturer usually specifies the ratio of water to dry grout. Damp-curing (see page 62) can increase the strength of the grout.

• *Latex-Portland cement grout* consists of cement and sand mixed with liquid latex instead of water. Its properties are similar to those of latex–Portland cement mortar. Follow the manufacturer's instructions for the ratio of dry mix to latex.

• *Sand-Portland cement grout* is mixed on the job, with water as the liquid. The ratio of cement to sand depends on the width of the spacing between tiles (see chart below). The increased proportion of sand gives a stronger mix. Up to $\frac{1}{5}$ part of lime is usually added to make the grout more workable.

Joint width	Cement	Sand
Less than $\frac{1}{8}$″	1 part	0 part
$\frac{1}{8}$″ to $\frac{1}{2}$″	1 part	2 parts
More than $\frac{1}{2}$″	1 part	3 parts

• *Commercial Portland cement grout* is a mixture of cement and other ingredients, formulated for grouting tiles on any surface. The wall type, usually white, is made with fine aggregates; tiles must be moistened if this grout is to be used. The floor type, which is gray, is used with mosaics, quarries, and pavers on both walls and floors. Both types must be damp-cured.

All cement-based grouts can be colored with materials available from your dealer. If your tiles are not glazed, however, test the colored grout before using; it may stain the tile.

Silicone rubber grout, sometimes called bathtub caulk, stays permanently flexible. It withstands extremes of cold and heat, repels water, and resists mildew. Available only in white and clear, it comes in tubes and cartridges. Pregrouted tile panels (see page 35) available from some manufacturers are grouted with silicone rubber.

Silicone rubber grout is most useful where surfaces tend to move slightly, as where a wall meets a floor or a counter top, or where tiles abut wood trim.

Epoxy-based grouts may be better than cement-based ones where resistance to chemicals is important, as in a darkroom. You may use epoxy grouts with any bonding agent. However, if your tiles are set in epoxy mortar or adhesive, you *must* use an epoxy grout. More expensive than all other grouts, epoxy grouts are water resistant. Working with them can be messy, and they are difficult to clean from tile surface once they have begun to harden. Their two components are mixed at the job site.

Epoxy grouts are available in black, dark brown, gray, and white. The white may yellow with age, however.

Epoxy grouts formulated for unglazed tile may contain a coarse silica fiber to increase bonding strength. The epoxy grouts formulated for glazed tile contain no such fiber, as it can scratch glazed surfaces.

Organic adhesive or mastic grouts are seldom used. They tend to wash out when subjected to heat.

Hiring a Licensed Contractor

You save a lot of time and effort by hiring a licensed professional tile contractor. A contractor can advise you in choosing tiles, furnish them, determine what kind of installation is most suitable, and perform a high-quality installation.

Many tiling projects you can perform yourself, but some require the experienced hand of a contractor. Swimming pool tile installation is not usually do-it-yourself work. Applications that require setting tiles in a full mortar bed, such as a free-form or sunken tub, are best handled by a pro. Tile dealers and distributors can give you the names of contractors in your area; the Yellow Pages also list them.

Helpful Tiling Tools

Most of the tools required for installing tile—ceramic, resilient, or wood—are general purpose tools you may already have. You'll recognize most of those shown below. A few are special tools used specifically for ceramic tile work.

A notched trowel for spreading adhesive is essential for any tiling project. Be sure to buy the correct trowel from the tile dealer when you buy the adhesive.

For ceramic tile installation, you will need a tile cutter and tile nippers to cut and shape tiles. Many tile dealers will loan or rent you the cutter and nippers. Or you can substitute a glass cutter and a combination square for the tile cutter and use slip-joint pliers for the nippers. (For a small charge, some dealers will cut tile you have marked.)

To apply grout between ceramic tiles, purchase a rubber-faced float. You can substitute a squeegee for this process, but it may not be as effective. Other tools you may need

for ceramic tile include a caulking gun, a cold chisel, and a center punch.

A saber saw or crosscut saw will come in handy if you must trim wood tiles or cut and install new underlayment panels (see page 69).

A rubber mallet is used to bed wood tiles into the adhesive. You can substitute a padded wooden block and hammer for this purpose.

When you're laying resilient tiles, use a utility knife to cut or shape the material.

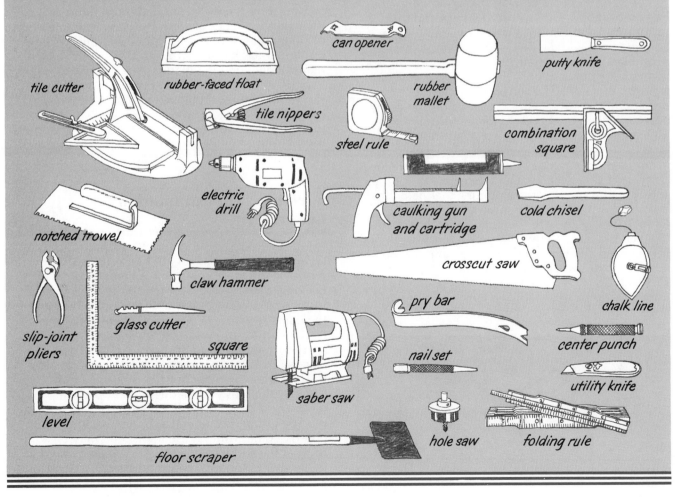

tile cutter — rubber-faced float — can opener — rubber mallet — putty knife — tile nippers — steel rule — combination square — notched trowel — electric drill — caulking gun and cartridge — cold chisel — claw hammer — crosscut saw — chalk line — slip-joint pliers — glass cutter — square — pry bar — saber saw — nail set — center punch — utility knife — level — hole saw — folding rule — floor scraper

Preparing the Surface

No matter which ceramic tile you choose or where you plan to install it, successful results require careful planning and meticulous preparation. On the next four pages, you'll find helpful information on planning your tile project as well as a guide to the selection, use, and preparation of the backing—the surface that will form the foundation for the tile.

You Need a Working Plan

Whether or not you hire a contractor, your tile project requires thorough planning. Start by outlining the sequence of steps you will follow. Involve your family in this; they will have to live with the disruptions involved, but they will also enjoy the results. This is most important if you're tiling a large, high-traffic area and if you do it in stages over a period of days. Whether you're tiling a kitchen, bath, or family room, your family's life style will be disrupted to some extent and you should plan accordingly.

Preparing the working area. Clear away rugs, furniture, and anything else that might get in the way. Cover adjacent finished areas with paper or plastic sheeting.

For walls. Remove base and shoe moldings and door and window trims. Most moldings and trims are attached with finishing nails; you can remove them in two ways. The first is to hammer a thin, broad-bladed pry bar gently behind the molding and pry carefully outward until that section of molding begins to move. Repeat the process a few inches further along until the entire molding or trim comes loose. A second method is to locate the nails and drive them through the molding with a narrow nailset.

You need not remove door casings—just tile up to the casing, leaving enough space for a grout joint. However, in some situations running the tile behind the casing will eliminate an awkward tile cut. Remove the casing with the same care that you removed the base. Then cut a rabbet in the back of the casing as shown below to allow room for the tile. You can do this with a router or a table saw.

For floors. Remove any doors that open into the room by tapping out the hinge pins (don't unscrew hinges). But, before you remove a door, use two tiles,

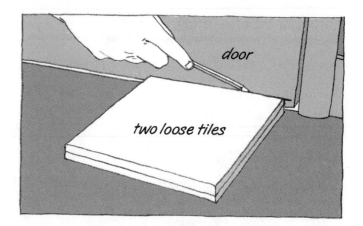

one on top of the other, as a guide to mark a line across its bottom. Cut the bottom off at this line before you rehang the door. If you don't wish to remove the base molding (in some older homes it may be impossible), just remove the shoe molding and then tile up to the base. In that case you should leave a grout joint between the base and the tiles.

In the bathroom or kitchen. You may need to remove accessories such as towel bars and paper holders from the walls. For bathroom floors, remove the vanity or pedestal wash basin and the toilet bowl (if floor-mounted). To tile bathroom walls, remove wall-mounted basins or toilets. (For removing and reinstalling plumbing fixtures, see the *Sunset* book *Basic Plumbing Illustrated.*) For tiling around a shower or bathtub, remove the faucet handles, escutcheons, spigots, and shower heads. Line the tub with cardboard to protect the finish and prevent debris from clogging the drain. Wrap masking tape around any exposed pipe threads.

Backings: The Foundation for Ceramic Tile

Of all the steps in successful tile installation, probably the most important is preparation of the backing, the material over which the tile will be installed. A thorough job of installing or preparing the backing will save you time and money later. Backings must be solid, flat, clean, and dry. Don't try to install tile over a springy surface. If the surface gives under pressure, reinforce or replace it. The surface you tile must be smooth and flat because the tiles will follow its contours. The chart on the next page shows the limits recommended by the Tile Council of America. If your backing doesn't come within these limits, you may be able to level the surface with a mastic underlayment or another compound recommended by the adhesive manufacturer. But if the surface is severely irregular,

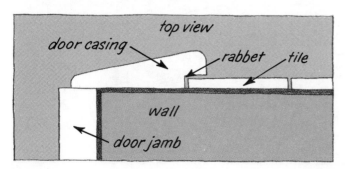

covering or replacing it with a new backing may be the only solution.

Surface	Adhesive	Must be flat within
All walls	All thin-sets	⅛″ in 8′
Concrete floor	Thin-set cement and epoxy	⅛″ in 10′
	Mastic	1⁄16″ in 3′
Wood floor*	Epoxy	⅛″ in 10′
	Mastic	1⁄16″ in 3′

*Adjacent edges of plywood subfloors must not be above or below each other by more than 1⁄32″.

Ceramic tiles can be laid on a variety of existing backings; if the old backing is unsatisfactory, one of several new backings may be used. These materials and their installation or preparation are described below.

New Backings

If you're going to install a new backing for your tile work, you have several materials to choose from. Your choice will depend on the location of the surface you'll be tiling and on the use the tiled surface will ultimately have.

Mortar bed, the traditional backing for ceramic tiles, is still the choice of many professionals, especially for areas that get wet.

A mortar bed is applied ¾″ to 1¼″ thick to ceilings, walls, floors, or counters. The mortar levels out the roughness and irregularities of the surface being covered and plumbs walls that are not vertical.

Unfortunately, the skills required to apply a mortar bed are beyond the abilities of most do-it-yourselfers. In addition, structural changes may be necessary to accommodate the thickness and weight of the mortar bed.

If your situation calls for a full mortar bed, you might have a plastering contractor do it for you. After the bed is finished, you can install the ceramic tiles at your leisure.

For the amateur, less demanding methods are available. Some of these work well in wet areas.

Gypsum wallboard is often used as a backing for ceramic tiles on walls. Because the gypsum core disintegrates if it becomes damp, standard gypsum wallboard should never be used in wet areas such as bathrooms. To install, use nails or adhesive to fasten the gypsum wallboard to existing walls or studs. Tape corners and joints and cover the nail heads. Use dry-set or latex–Portland cement mortars or mastic as adhesives for ceramic tile on gypsum wallboard (see page 39).

Water-resistant gypsum wallboard was developed as a tile backing for wet areas such as tub enclosures and showers. The gypsum core is treated to make it water resistant. To avoid confusion with standard gypsum board, the water-resistant paper face of the panels is colored, usually blue or green.

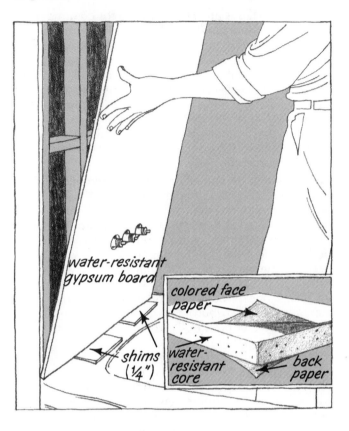

This type of gypsum board should be applied directly to the studs with nails or adhesive. Using special joint compound according to the instructions of the gypsum board manufacturer, tape all joints between panels, cover all nail heads, and seal all cut edges. With water-resistant gypsum wallboard, use type I mastic, which is water-resistant, for setting the tile.

Plywood is often laid over existing plank or plywood subfloors as a backing for ceramic tiles. The plywood should be exterior or underlayment grade, at least ⅜″ thick. Place the panels on the subfloor, staggering them so that four corners do not line up (see page 70). Leave a gap of 1/32″ between adjacent panels (¼″ if you intend to use an epoxy adhesive). Nail panels to subfloor with 6-penny ring-shank nails spaced 6″ apart.

Directly over joists, you can use exterior grade plywood (⅝″ thick if Group 1, ¾″ if Group 2— see your lumber dealer) as a combination subfloor and tile backing. Joists must be 16″ or less over centers; fasten plywood with adhesive or 6-penny ring-shank nails spaced 6″ apart. Set panels at right angles to joists; back unsupported panel joints with 2 by 4s.

(Continued on next page)

. . . Continued from page 43

Plywood may also serve as backing for tile counters. Exterior-grade plywood ¾"-thick should be installed over a solid support so it does not give under pressure.

On both floors and counters, the preferred adhesives for plywood backings are organic adhesives and epoxies.

A concrete slab is an excellent base for ceramic tiles, both indoors and out. The concrete must be completely cured and free from cracks, waxy or oily films, and curing compounds. If you must pour a new concrete slab as a base for ceramic tile, consult a concrete contractor. Be sure that a waterproof membrane is placed over the ground before the slab is poured. Any movement or cracking of the slab will immediately affect the ceramic tile, so the concrete should be reinforced with metal rods or mesh.

Backer board, technically called concrete glass-fiber-reinforced backer board, is a recently developed material that combines some desirable qualities of a mortar bed with the installation ease of gypsum wallboard or plywood. Next to a mortar bed, it is the preferred backing in wet areas, because the backer board is unaffected by water. Although it may be difficult to find in some localities, backer board can be ordered through a ceramic tile distributor (see the Yellow Pages). Use only dry-set or latex–Portland cement mortar to bond ceramic tile to backer board (these materials are discussed on page 39).

Backer board is fastened with 1½" galvanized roofing nails directly to wall studs or over existing wall surfaces. Seal joints between panels and between panel and tub or shower receptor, as well as any other openings, with either of the above mortars. Tape corners with 2"-wide coated fiberglass tape embedded in a thin coat of mortar.

Backer board can also be installed over plywood subfloors at least ½" thick on joists that are spaced no more than 16" from center to center. Fasten the backer board to the subfloor with construction adhesive and 1½" galvanized roofing nails. Fill gaps between the panels with the same mortar used to set the tiles.

Existing Backings

You can install ceramic tile directly over many existing backings, such as wood, sprayed-on plastic coatings, seamless resilient floors, plastic laminates, vinyl and asphalt tiles, ceramic tiles, and concrete.

Be sure that the surfaces are sound, clean, flat (see chart on page 43), and properly prepared. Make certain that you use the correct adhesive. If the existing surface is badly cracked or broken, loose, irregular, or otherwise in poor condition, replace it or cover it with a new backing.

The backings described here are the more common ones. Always follow the recommendations of the adhesive manufacturer; if you're in doubt, discuss the situation with your tile supplier.

Gypsum wallboard. Clean dirt and grease from gypsum board walls with a household cleaner. Remove any loose or flaking paint; roughen the finish if it's glossy. Sanding will do both jobs. Fill any cracks, gouges, or holes with a mastic underlayment recommended by the adhesive manufacturer. Remove any wallpaper from the wallboard. (If you don't, the weight of the tiles will peel off the wallpaper.) Use only mastic to bond ceramic tiles to existing gypsum wallboard.

Wood surfaces. Planks or plywood, if rigid, can be used as backing for ceramic tile. Old finishes should be roughened or removed and the wood sanded flat if it is uneven (see chart on page 43). You can use an organic adhesive, if it is compatible, on any finish that remains. However, if you intend to lay the tile with epoxy, remove *all* of the old finish.

Resilient floors. Tiled or seamless resilient floors and plastic laminates, if rigid (not cushioned) and sound, make good backings for ceramic tile.

Depending on the material, the appropriate adhesive may be mastic or epoxy. To lay ceramic tile over a vinyl floor, you should use epoxy adhesive though a *good* mastic works, whereas over plastic laminates you may use either mastic or epoxy. Check with your tile dealer and the adhesive manufacturer for their recommendations.

Concrete subfloor. An existing concrete subfloor must be flat, smooth, dry, clean, and free of cracks before ceramic tiles can be installed. You can remove grease and oil stains with a chemical garage floor cleaner obtainable at most auto supply stores. Chip or scrape off any excess concrete, globs of paint, or other foreign material. If the concrete surface is glossy, effloresced, sealed, or painted, roughen it by chipping or sanding or have it sandblasted by a contractor. Probably the easiest method for a do-it-yourselfer is to sand the floor down to bare concrete with a floor sander and #4 or #5 open-cut sandpaper. Finish by scouring with a stiff bristle or wire brush and vacuuming up all loose material.

If you plan to use a cement-based mortar as the adhesive, fill all the holes, low areas, cracks, and expansion joints in the concrete with a good

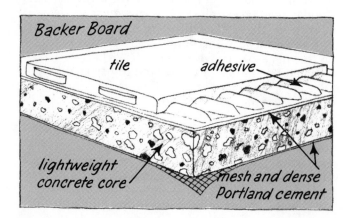

Backer Board

tile   adhesive

lightweight concrete core   mesh and dense Portland cement

concrete patching material. If you use mastic, you can do the repair work with a mastic underlayment, which is somewhat easier to apply. When this work is finished, your floor must be flat (see chart on page 43).

If your concrete floor is rough, uneven, or otherwise in poor condition, you can have a new concrete floor installed over it or use a mortar bed as a backing for the tile.

Ceramic tile. Existing ceramic tile and some masonry tiles may be used as backing for new ceramic tiles. The existing tiles must be well bonded and clean when you apply the adhesive. And make sure that the existing tiles are not loose. Remove any loose tiles and scrape the old adhesive off the tile's back and the wall. Butter the back with a similar adhesive and press the tile back in place.

In wet areas such as shower stalls, loose tiles often indicate that water has penetrated into the backing. Remove loose tiles and examine the backing behind or beneath them; don't be surprised if you find the soggy remains of regular gypsum board behind wall tiles. Even if no tiles are loose, check the grout carefully. Broken or missing grout is evidence that water has penetrated behind the tiles, weakening the bond and damaging the backing. In either case, the best remedy is to tear out the old backing and replace it with water-resistant gypsum board or backer board. Repairing the damaged spots might solve the problem for a while, but eventually you will have trouble.

If you are satisfied that there is no water damage, or if you are working in a dry area, clean the tile. If you had to reset some tiles in the existing surface, wait until the adhesive on those tiles is dry. Remove any scum, mineral buildup, coatings, wax, and dirt from the old tiles. To do this, use an abrasive disc mounted on an electric drill. The disc will also roughen the surface for better adhesion. Finish up by rinsing with clear water.

One more factor to consider in planning the new tile is whether to stop at the height of the existing tile or continue up to the ceiling. Cover the edge of the old tile with cove or a cove and bullnose cap. To tile to the ceiling, install new backing above the old tile. Shim the backing, if necessary, to make it flush with the old tile. In damp areas, use water-resistant gypsum board or backer board.

You may use any of the thin-set adhesives described on page 39 over existing tile. If you installed any new backing, be sure to choose an appropriate adhesive.

You May Need to Prime or Seal

The manufacturer of the adhesive you choose may recommend that the backing be primed or sealed before tile is applied. By penetrating the backing, the primer or sealer (sometimes known as a bonderizer) accomplishes two things: 1) it increases the water resistance of the backing, and 2) it strengthens the bond between the backing and the tile.

The primer or sealer may be a thin coat of the adhesive or a special material prepared by the adhesive manufacturer. To determine whether or not to prime or seal your backing, read the information on the container of your adhesive.

Is Your Concrete Floor Dry?

A flat, interior concrete slab makes an excellent backing for all types of tile—as long as it remains dry. A damp slab causes most tile adhesives to deteriorate and makes resilient and wood tiles swell, buckle, or rot. Although the builder may have waterproofed the slab by placing a polyethylene barrier on the ground before pouring the concrete, you have no way of knowing for sure. Unless such a waterproof shield is present, moisture can be drawn in through the concrete to the surface.

Just after a rainstorm, when the ground is saturated with water, is the best time to test a slab for dampness. To make the test, scatter several 1' squares of polyethylene film (food wrap available at supermarkets works well) over the slab.

Fasten the four edges of each square to the slab with cloth tape to make an airtight seal.

Check the squares after 24 hours. If the undersides of the polyethylene squares are fogged with moisture, the slab is too wet to lay tile on.

If persistent moisture is evident, call in professional help. The Yellow Pages are a good source. For resilient or wood tile work, look under "Floor Laying, Refinishing, & Resurfacing." For ceramic tile work, look under "Tile—Ceramic, Contractors." If the bases of the walls are wet as well as the slab, your problem may be serious enough to require a water-proofing specialist. See the listings under "Waterproofing Contractors" or "Concrete Contractors."

Here are four solutions a professional may offer for keeping your slab's surface dry:

1) Lay drain tile in a ditch around your house.

2) Lay a sheet of polyethylene on top of your slab, then cover it with another concrete slab at least 1" thick.

3) Spread "cold-applied cut-back" asphalt across the slab, then press overlapping polyethylene strips into the asphalt. This procedure is appropriate only if you'll be installing wood tiles.

4) Trowel a commercially prepared, latex-based waterproofing compound onto the slab. However, these compounds are generally unavailable to homeowners for do-it-yourself application.

How to Install Ceramic Tile

On the preceding pages you've learned what kinds of tile are available; where tile is appropriate; how to plan for, select, and buy tile; how to prepare various backings; what kinds of adhesives to use; and which kinds of grout to apply. This section will take you through some basic tiling projects: a floor, a wall, a bathtub enclosure, a shower, a counter top, and such finishing touches as a window sill or a fireplace facing and hearth.

Test your layout. You will have to adapt each project to your own unique situation. For this reason, always make a "dry run" by laying out tiles on the surface you are covering. If that surface is vertical, mark out a similar area on the floor. This dry run will enable you to anticipate any problems, decide where to cut tiles, and locate the trim pieces. Always arrange the tile layout so cut tiles are in the least noticeable corners.

A few pointers. If you intend to install tile both on walls and floor, as in a bathroom, tile all the walls before the floor. This is necessary if you're using cove tile at the bottom of the wall. Even if you're not using cove, this sequence is still more convenient. Of the walls, start with the tub enclosure—the wall area around the tub.

When using a mixture of decorative and plain tiles, be sure to place the decorative tiles high enough to be visible, not hidden behind furniture. Once the adhesive has set, you can't change your mind.

Applying the adhesive. Study the directions supplied by the manufacturer of your adhesive. These will tell you how the material should be mixed and what size notches the trowel should have. These will also give the open time—the length of time you have to work with the adhesive after spreading. Also refer to the section on adhesives, beginning on page 39. If you are using a mastic with a solvent base, remember to ventilate the working area well.

All the thin-set adhesives are applied in basically the same way. The tool used is a trowel with notches or serrations along one side and one end. First, spread the adhesive over the backing, using the smooth edges of the trowel to form a thin layer. Then, with the trowel held at a 45° angle to the surface, comb the layer of adhesive with the notched edges of the trowel. Press the trowel firmly against the backing so the adhesive forms ridges as you comb. The valleys between them will be covered with only a thin film.

Spread only the amount of adhesive you can cover before it sets. The height and width of the ridges your trowel forms determines how thick the bonding layer will be after the tile is bedded in the adhesive. Because the optimum thickness varies with both the type of tile and the adhesive, the adhesive manufacturer specifies the size of trowel notches

that should be used. When spreading epoxies, be sure to force the material into the gaps between plywood panels.

How to space tiles. Floor tiles and many wall tiles come without lugs to space the joints. You can maintain uniform spacing between tiles with other methods, though. For joints wider than 1/16", you might use molded spacers (see page 32) available from many tile suppliers. Scraps of plywood (see page 49) of appropriate thickness work well with ¼" or wider joints. For the narrow joints usually associated with wall tiles, you might use finishing nails (see page 53). Still another method—usable for joints of any size—is shown below.

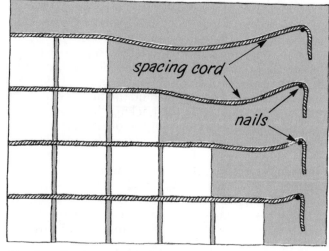

Spacing tiles in traditional way uses cord or rope. As you set each course, lay damp cord of desired size on top of tiles. Remove after adhesive sets.

A straightedge made from a good piece of 1" by 4" lumber is handy for laying out the job, aligning tile, and—if marked as shown below—adjusting tile spacing.

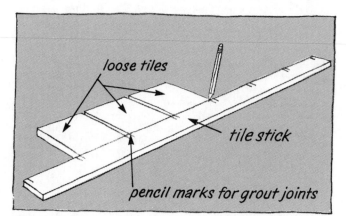

Tile stick with a straight edge can be used to lay and space tiles. Use 1" by 3" or 1" by 4" lumber marked with proper spacing for grout joints.

(Continued on page 48)

Marking and Cutting Ceramic Tiles

Wherever you're tiling, you will need parts of tiles to cover the area completely.

Though many tile dealers will cut tile for you with a diamond saw, making trips to the dealer may be inconvenient, especially if your tiling job is complicated. Even though ceramic tiles are thick and hard, you can cut them without too much difficulty. Your dealer can loan or rent you the special tools required.

Marking the cut. If your tiles have ridged backs, make cuts parallel to the ridges. To mark for straight cuts, place tile, finished surface up, exactly on top of the last full tile

you set (see page 78). Then place another tile on top of this one, with one edge butted against the wall. Using the edge of the top tile as a guide, mark the cut-off line with a fine felt-tip pen.

To mark a tile for a corner, use the above process twice—once on each wall.

To fit a tile to an irregular contour, cut a pattern from cardboard and then transfer the contour to the tile. Where a pipe comes through the tile, as in tubs and showers, don't do anything until all the other field tiles are in place. Then either measure the location of the required hole or hold the tile

against the pipe and mark the hole (see drawing on page 57). The escutcheons will hide any minor inaccuracies. To cut the hole, you have two choices. You can use a hole saw and an electric drill, or you can cut the tile in two and then nibble away the waste material.

Cutting tile. Shown below are the common methods of cutting tile. **Be sure to wear safety goggles when cutting tile.**

Smoothing edges. After a tile is broken or nipped, it may have projections on the cut edge. Remove these by rubbing against a whetstone and water or against the rough surface of a concrete block.

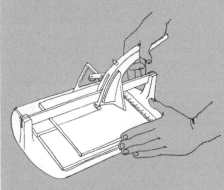

Score surface *with tile cutter. Downward pressure on handle will break tile along scored mark.*

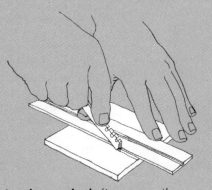

Another method: *first score tile with glass cutter guided by straightedge or square . . .*

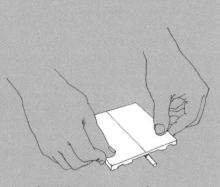

. . . then place *score mark directly over nail, wire, or dowel. Press down evenly on both edges.*

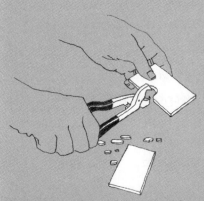

Tile nippers *cut tiles to irregular shapes. Scoring cutoff line with glass cutter helps.*

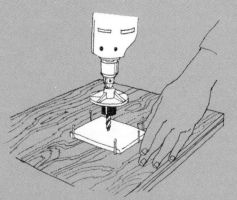

To cut hole *in tile, use hole saw mounted in electric drill. Or nibble two halves using previous drawing as a guide.*

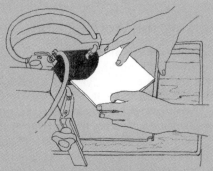

Tile dealers *will cut marked tiles for you at nominal cost with water-cooled diamond cutoff wheel.*

Installing Tiles on the Floor

Floors are among the easier tiling projects for the do-it-yourselfer. This is because the tiles are set on a horizontal surface, so gravity is on your side. Once you set a tile, its weight holds it in place. This section gives you some preparation reminders and discusses laying out the job, actually setting the tiles, and adding the finishing touches.

Preparation

Before you begin, be sure to read the section on preparing the surface (see page 42). The backing for a ceramic tile floor must be rigid, flat, smooth, clean, and dry.

Materials. Check the tiles, adhesive, and grout you purchased. Do the tile colors match from box to box? Slight variations sometimes occur. These variations are one of the charms of tile—but if you prefer uniformity, exchange the tiles. Is the adhesive compatible with your backing? Will the grout work with the adhesive and tiles you have? Answer these questions now rather than after you have laid most of the tiles.

Many tiles, particularly those with reddish bodies, tend to be dusty. This dust can prevent adhesives from bonding to the tiles, so wash and dry them, if necessary, before use.

Plan for doorways. Where tile stops in a doorway or similar opening, there is often a difference in height between the tile surface and the adjoining floor. If the tile is higher, you can finish off the edge with bullnose tiles. These have a curved edge that creates smooth transition between the two levels. When a tile floor meets a carpeted area, the levels may be roughly the same, so the regular square-edged tiles may do the job. With mosaic tile a marble saddle is often used to make a transition between two levels. These are available from most tile distributors.

Marking the Working Lines

Take the time to plan the job carefully and establish accurate working lines. Doing this will save you time and effort and give you a ceramic tile floor that will be admired by all.

Two basic methods are used to establish working lines. In one you start laying tiles in the center of the room; in the other you start at one end. If you have picked tiles such as ogee or Moorish that are not square or rectangular, you may have to make some adjustments in the working lines. Make a dry-run to determine what problems you may encounter, before you open the adhesive. If you need help, consult your tile dealer or distributor.

Working from the center. This method is also used for laying resilient and wood tiles. The layout of

working lines and the tiling sequence for this method are described on pages 70 and 71. This method usually results in cut tiles along all four walls.

If your room is out of square or if you've chosen a decorative design or pattern that should be symmetrically located in the room, you will probably wish to start in the center. If you do, nail wooden battens along the working lines to help keep the tiles straight.

Starting at the wall. Many professional tile setters use this method, which has its roots in the traditional way of setting tile on a damp mortar bed. Out of necessity, tile setters worked from one end to avoid disturbing the carefully leveled mortar bed. Many professional tile setters use this method even if the room is not square and the walls are irregular. To avoid unnecessary complications, however, consider using this method only if at least two adjoining straight walls meet at exactly 90° angles. When you use this method with such a room, usually only two sides of the room will be lined with cut tiles.

Check the room for square corners and straight walls by placing a tile tight against the walls in each corner. Stretch your chalk line along the outside edges of each pair of tiles, pull tight, and snap. Variations in the distance between chalk mark and wall will show any crookedness in the wall. Some variation—about the width of a grout joint— can be tolerated. With a framing square, check that the lines at each corner intersect at right angles. Either straight wall adjoining a square corner can be your starting point. The other wall will help keep the tiles in straight lines.

Making a dry run—laying the tiles out on the floor—can help you determine the best layout and

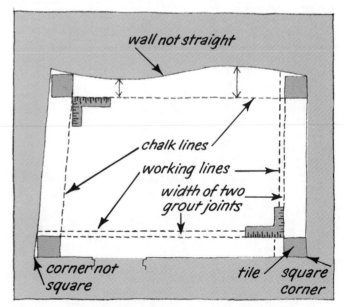

You can start laying floor tiles *from one wall even if corners are not square or wall not straight. When two adjacent walls are straight and form a square corner, you'll find job easier.*

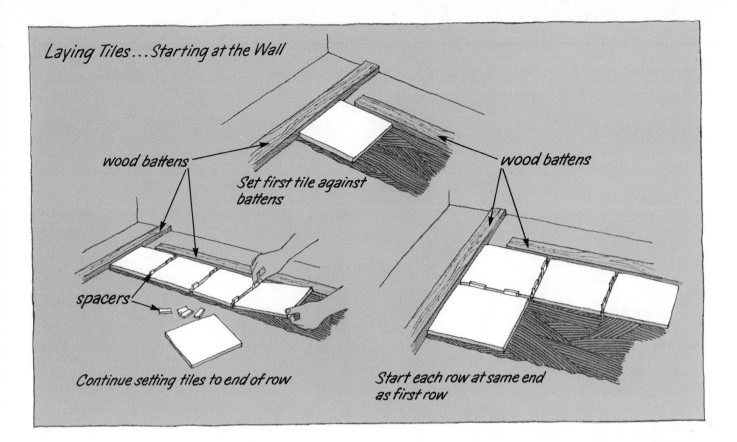

Laying Tiles...Starting at the Wall

wood battens

Set first tile against battens

wood battens

spacers

Continue setting tiles to end of row

Start each row at same end as first row

minimize the number of cut tiles. Make sure you allow space for grout joints. A tile stick (see page 46) can help you achieve uniform spacing. Sometimes a slight alteration of grout joint widths can eliminate a row of cut tiles. Whatever cut tiles you have will be less conspicuous if your layout places them where furniture will at least partially hide them.

To locate the working lines, use the chalked lines on the floor as a guide. Your working lines should allow for slight variations in the straightness of the walls (about the width of a grout joint) and for the grout joint between the first and second rows of tile. Select the walls you wish to use as guides and pick one of them to begin on. Then, on the side of the line away from the wall, mark another line parallel to the first and spaced a distance equal to the width of two grout joints. Repeat this with the chalk line along the other wall. These are your working lines.

Nail a wood straightedge or batten (1″ by 2″ or 1″ by 3″) along each of the working lines. These will give you rigid guides to butt the tiles against. Make sure the two battens form a right angle. If they don't, check your measurements and adjust as needed.

Laying the Tiles

Now you are ready to start putting ceramic tiles on the floor. Spread a strip of adhesive on the floor along one of the battens with the notched trowel recommended by your adhesive manufacturer. Spread only as much as you can cover before the adhesive begins to set. Start with about 1 square yard. As you become more proficient at laying tiles, you can spread adhesive over a larger area.

Place the first tile, with a gentle twisting motion, into the corner formed by the two battens. Make sure the tile is butted tightly against the battens. With the same motion, place the second tile alongside the first. As floor tiles seldom have molded-in spacers, use a molded spacer or a piece of wood of the right thickness to establish the width of the grout joint. The molded spacers can be left in or removed before you grout. Remove wood spacers after the adhesive has begun to set. As you go along, clean off any adhesive that gets on the surface of the tiles. This is especially important with epoxies. After an epoxy has set, you will not be able to remove it from the tile surface.

Continue setting tiles and spacers along the batten until you reach the other end of the room. If necessary, mark and cut the last tile as described on page 47. Instead of having all the joints lined up, you might prefer the running bond used in the quarry tile floor shown on page 6. Just start the second row—and every second row thereafter—with the first tile spaced one-half the width of a tile from the batten that goes the length of the room.

Whichever bond you choose, begin the second row from the same end of the room as the first one. Measure and cut the last tile as required. As you work toward the other end of the room, slide a block of padded wood, large enough to cover several tiles, over the tiles while you tap it with a hammer. This process, called "beating-in," beds the tiles in the adhesive and makes them level with each other.

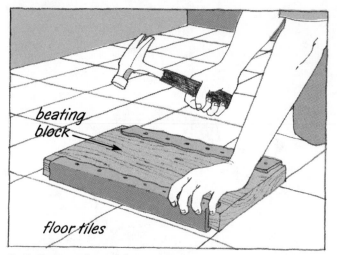

Bed tiles *in adhesive by tapping on length of padded lumber or plywood while sliding it over tiles. Smooth, even surface results.*

Try to stay off the surface of the tiles as you work. If you must walk on them, lay down pieces of plywood as steppingstones.

From time to time, check with your square and straightedge to make sure the courses are straight. If some of the tiles are out of line, don't panic. Just wiggle them into position.

When your rows of tile have covered the whole room, mark, cut, and set the last row. After beating these in, check back and make sure that you have cleaned all the adhesive from the tiles.

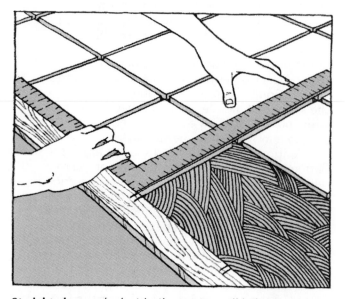

Straightedge *marked with tile spacing will help you maintain straight courses and even spacings. Check with square often to assure professional look.*

Next, carefully remove the battens and spread adhesive over the area not yet tiled. Begin laying the border tiles in the same corner you started in. Work toward the ends, beating in the tiles as you move along. If you laid out your working lines properly, you won't have to cut these tiles. When you have finished, clean off the surface of the tiles.

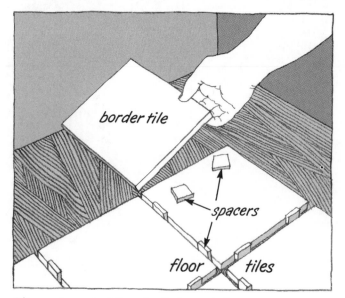

After main part *of floor is tiled, carefully remove battens. Spread adhesive on remaining floor and set border tiles.*

Stay off the tiles at least overnight—longer if recommended by the adhesive manufacturer. Keep all but essential traffic off the floor until you grout the joints. Tiles can break very easily prior to grouting. After the adhesive has fully set (see page 62), you can begin grouting.

Finishing Up

Wait until the adhesive dries before applying grout (see page 62). The solvent fumes from mastic can form bubbles in the grout and even discolor it.

Remove any remaining spacers, clean adhesive from the tile surface, and reread the information about grouts beginning on page 40. Also remove any excess adhesive or debris from the joints; otherwise the grout may crack or fail to bond in those areas. After the adhesive has dried, apply the grout as described on page 62.

After the grout is fully cured, wash the surface with detergent or household cleaner and water. When your new tile floor is completely dry, seal the grout as described on page 63.

While the grout is curing, replace the base and shoe moldings. Do any necessary cutting of door bottoms and reinstall the doors.

There you have it—a ceramic tile floor you can be proud of.

Installing Tiles on Walls

Decorating a straight wall with ceramic tile is relatively easy. If your wall has breaks or openings, however, you may find the job somewhat more difficult. In any event, if you proceed carefully and methodically you can create a tiled wall that will give pleasure for many years.

Preparing the Surface

Remove faceplates for electrical switches and outlets, bathroom accessories, and anything else attached to the wall.

If your project includes adding electrical outlets or installing a recessed cabinet, now is the time to do the work inside the wall. The *Sunset* books *Basic Carpentry Illustrated* and *Basic Home Wiring Illustrated* provide valuable information for these projects.

The wall surface must be firm, dry, clean, and flat. It can be of any of the materials described under "Existing Backings" on page 44. Remove any wallpaper; it may loosen and peel off, taking your new tiles with it. Be sure to clean off dirt and grease and roughen shiny areas. Painted surfaces are acceptable as long as the paint is not flaking. If the surface seems porous, follow the recommendations of the adhesive manufacturer regarding priming or sealing.

Marking the Working Lines

Accurate working lines will help you keep the tiles properly aligned—giving your completed tile work an elegant and professional look.

The horizontal line. This line should be near the bottom of the wall, because tiling up is usually easier than tiling down.

For bathroom walls, extend the horizontal line for the tub (see drawing, page 54) onto these walls. Then measure down a full number of tiles (you can use your tile stick), leaving at least a full tile width above the floor. Then mark the horizontal working line through this point with a straightedge and level. You can also use the top of the last full tile at the bottom of the leg.

For other walls, find the lowest point by setting the level on the floor at various locations against the walls to be tiled. At the lowest point, place a tile against the wall (see drawing, right); mark its top edge on the wall. If the installation will have a cove base, set a cove tile on the floor and a wall tile above it (allow for a grout joint). Mark the top of the wall tile. Using the level, the straightedge, and the mark, draw a horizontal line across the wall. Extend this line onto the other walls to be tiled.

After marking your horizontal working lines, nail battens (1" by 2" strips will do) to the walls. Their top edges should be on the lines.

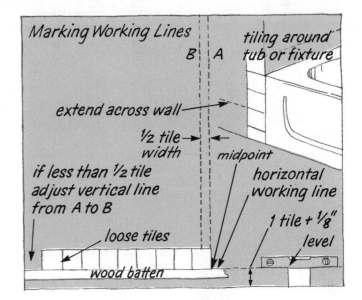

Marking Working Lines — tiling around tub or fixture. extend across wall. ½ tile width. if less than ½ tile adjust vertical line from A to B. midpoint. horizontal working line. 1 tile + ⅛". level. loose tiles. wood batten.

The vertical lines. Locate the midpoint of a wall and mark it on the horizontal line (see drawing above). Starting at this midpoint, measure with the tile stick or set a row of loose tiles on the batten to determine the size of the tiles at the ends of the wall. If they will be less than half a tile, move your midpoint mark one-half tile to avoid narrow pieces of tile. Then use the level and straightedge to mark a vertical line on the wall through your mark. Repeat the process with the other walls.

Some final hints. If the tile won't go all the way to the ceiling, you will want to mark the point at which it stops. Usually a tile wainscot extends to a height of 4' to 5'. With your tile stick, mark on the vertical line the top of the uppermost tile—plus the bullnose or cap—that falls within these limits. With your level, mark a horizontal line through this point across the wall. Repeat the process for the other walls.

For bathroom walls, lay out the locations of ceramic towel bars, paper holders, and soap and toothbrush holders. Be sure to leave these areas open when you set the tiles.

Setting the Tile

Whether you set the tiles with the joints lined up—known as jack-on-jack—or staggered in a running bond, refer to the appropriate tiling sequence on page 53. If you want a running bond, center the first tile on the vertical line. Then set the succeeding tiles in the sequence shown, maintaining the step pattern as you cover the wall. For the more common jack-on-jack bond, read on.

Set the first tile on the batten with one side aligned exactly with the vertical line. Use a slight twist as you place the tile; don't slide it. Sliding will push adhesive into the joints, preventing proper

(Continued on page 53)

Replacing Damaged Tiles

If one of your tiles becomes damaged with use, you can replace it by following steps 1 through 9 below. Often, though, one or more tiles may loosen and require resetting. **Resetting loose tiles.** Loose tiles are easy to reset. Start by scraping all traces of old adhesive and grout from the tile and the backing surface. Then follow steps 5 through 9, outlined below. **Matching replacement tiles.** If you don't have spare tiles from the original installation, you may have trouble finding an exact match. Many tile dealers and contractors have "bone piles" where they keep old, discontinued, and slightly flawed tiles. When looking for replacements, always carry along a sample of the original tile, if possible.

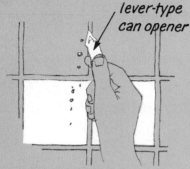

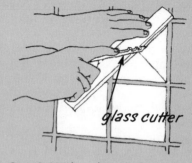

Step 1. *Remove grout from joints around damaged tile with a lever-type can opener. (Skip this step if grout joints are more than ⅛" wide.)*

Step 2. *Punch hole through center of damaged tile with hammer and center punch or nail set. Be careful not to damage surface behind.*

Step 3. *With a glass cutter, score a deep X across the face of the tile, through the center hole.*

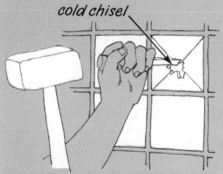

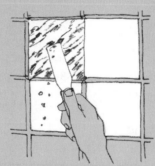

Step 4. *Starting at the center, chip out old tile and remaining grout with a soft-headed hammer and cold chisel, using light, rapid blows.*

Step 5. *Clean area behind tile, removing all old adhesive and grout. Use sandpaper to smooth edges and rough spots.*

Step 6. *If necessary, fill and smooth backing with patching plaster to level new tile. When plaster dries, paint with latex primer.*

Step 7. *When primer dries, apply mastic to back of new tile with putty knife. Keep adhesive ½" away from edges of tile.*

Step 8. *With a hammer and block of wood, gently tap tile in place until level. Wait 24 hours before grouting.*

Step 9. *Apply grout by wiping into joints with a damp rag or sponge. Use finger to smooth grout joints. Clean off excess.*

. . . Continued from page 51

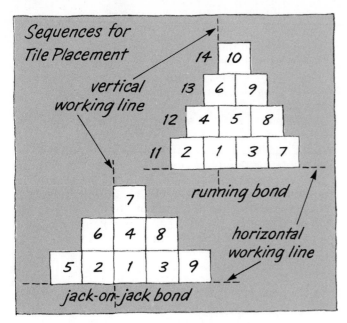

Sequences for Tile Placement

vertical working line

running bond

horizontal working line

jack-on-jack bond

from their boxes. After you have cut and fit tiles around the boxes, remount the outlets and switches. If you need longer screws, get some 6-32 FH machine screws from a hardware store. Check the length you need before making the trip.

Corners require special attention. The tiles in an inside corner butt against each other. On outside corners, set one column with bullnose tiles so that the bullnose covers the unfinished edges of the tiles on the adjoining wall. Windows also pose corner problems. If one of your walls contains a window, finish off the sides and sill with bullnose tiles cut to fit.

Wait for the adhesive to set. Then carefully remove the battens and—if you used them—the finishing nails. Twist the nails as you pull them out. Now you are ready to set tiles along the bottom of the wall. Cut the tiles to fit. Spread adhesive on the bare wall, and then set the tiles in place. Be sure to beat in these tiles.

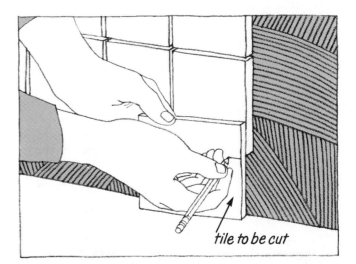

tile to be cut

Mark tiles *for the bottom row after removing batten. Be sure to allow for the grout joint at the base.*

alignment of the tile. Set the succeeding tiles in the same manner, following the sequence illustrated. If your tiles have no spacing lugs, you can use 6-penny finishing nails as shown below or cords (see page 46).

Continue setting the tiles upward and toward the ends, maintaining the pyramid pattern. After laying several tiles, beat them in by sliding a piece of plywood across the tiles as you tap it with a hammer. When you reach the ends of each row, cut the tiles to fit (see page 47). For the top course (row), use either bullnose or cap tiles to finish off the top of the tiled surface. If you're tiling to the ceiling, cut the last course to fit if necessary.

If the area you're tiling contains any electrical outlets or switches, turn off the power to them. Remove the mounting screws and pull the devices

Now check your work. If any tiles are out of alignment, wiggle them into position. You have plenty of time, since the adhesive dries slowly once the tiles are in place. Clean any adhesive from the face of the tiles and from the grout joints. While the adhesive is drying, install any flush-mounted accessories with the same adhesive. Tape these in place while they dry. If you're using mastic, try the floor type. It dries faster and makes a stronger bond.

Finishing Up

The next step is filling the joints with grout. Information about grouts and their characteristics begins on page 40. After the adhesive has dried, grout the joints as described on page 62. Allow the grout to cure completely before applying sealer to the grout (see page 63).

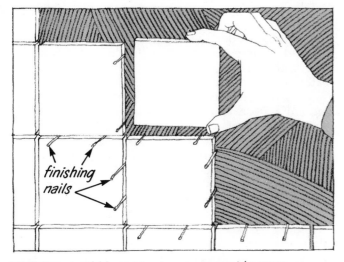

finishing nails

Wall tiles *should be set in step, or pyramid pattern. Place each with a slight twist; do not slide. Use 6-penny finishing nails to space tiles with no lugs.*

Tiling a Tub Enclosure

Especially in an older house, tiling around a tub is a fairly difficult do-it-yourself project, though it is often a first project. Water damage and deterioration of the bond and backing, and color schemes that have become outdated are frequent reasons for remodeling. If you plan carefully and proceed methodically, you too can restore your tub enclosure to pristine beauty.

Preparation

First, cover the drain and line your tub with cardboard to prevent damage. Dropping even a small tool can chip the enamel finish. Remove such fixtures as soap dishes, grabs, and towel bars, and take the handles and escutcheons from the faucets. Wrap masking tape around exposed threads to protect them.

Wet areas, such as those around a tub, require extra care. This project will take quite a bit of time, so do a thorough job of surface preparation—even replace the backing if needed. Your effort will pay off in a tile job that will be functional and beautiful for years.

Study the section on new and existing backings beginning on page 42. Carefully check the tile around your tub. Are tiles tightly bonded? If not, remove the loose tiles and examine the backing. If no water damage is present, glue the tiles back in place with water-resistant mastic. Then clean and prepare all the surfaces to be covered with tile, as described on page 44.

If bond and backing have been damaged by water, installing a new backing will save you time, effort and—in the long run—money. Refer to the section on new backings beginning on page 43 and the drawing at the bottom of page 58.

The preferred backing for wet areas is cement mortar. But unless you have plastered with cement mortar and worked with tile, you may want to leave this method to the pros. The other two materials suggested for this application, backer board and water-resistant gypsum wallboard, should give you little difficulty.

Marking the Working Lines

Accurate, carefully established working lines will help you impart a professional appearance to your completed enclosure. Without accurate lines, the courses (rows) will not be level and the tiles in the columns will not line up.

Horizontal working line. The way this line is established depends on whether or not your tub is level (see drawing at right).

If the tub is level to within ⅛", most professionals locate the horizontal working line from the high point of the tub lip. This method uses only full tiles in the bottom course. The slight variation in gap between the tiles and the tub is obscured when the gap is caulked.

After you have located the high point of the tub lip with your level, measure up the width of one tile plus ⅛". Mark a level line on the wall through this point. Then, with your level and a straight piece of wood, extend this line carefully around the ends and back of the tub. If the adjoining walls are to be tiled as well, extend the horizontal working line to them.

If the tub is not level to within ⅛", locate the horizontal line from the low point; otherwise the gap between the top and the bottom of the tiles will be excessive. Then proceed as explained above. Note that you will have to cut the bottom row of tiles to fit.

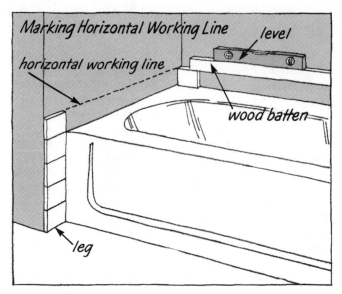

Mark *horizontal working line on back wall at one tile plus ⅛" up from tub lip. Extend to end walls.*

The vertical working lines. These lines can also be located in more than one way. This is particularly true of the walls at the ends of the tub, where the extent of the surface to be tiled may vary.

The back wall is where you start in setting tile around a tub. Some tile setters work from the more visible end of the wall to the less visible, cutting tiles to fit into the less obtrusive corner. The effect is usually more pleasing, however, if you center the tiles so that those at each end are of equal width.

Locate the midpoint of the back wall and mark it on your horizontal working line. Either use your tile stick (see page 46) or lay a row of loose tiles along the back of the tub to determine the size of the end tiles. (Be sure that a joint is lined up on the center mark.) If the end tiles will be larger than half a tile, mark the vertical working line

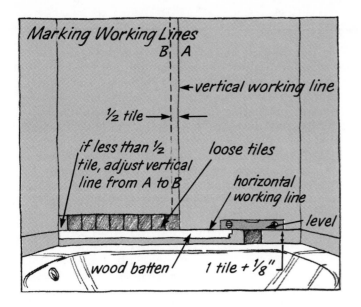

Marking Working Lines

B A

← vertical working line

½ tile →

if less than ½ tile, adjust vertical line from A to B

loose tiles

horizontal working line

← level

wood batten

1 tile + ⅛"

through the midpoint with your level and a straightedge.

If the end tile size is less than half a tile, then mark the vertical working line exactly one-half tile to one side or the other of the midpoint. This adjustment avoids narrow end tiles, which are harder to cut and less attractive than larger ones.

The end walls are usually laid out after the back wall is covered with tile. Position your vertical working line to minimize the number of cut tiles and to locate them in a corner. If you have a newer tub and are using 4⅛" square tiles, you might get away without cutting any tiles. (The height and width of these tubs are multiples of the 4⅛" tiles.)

The illustration below shows typical positions of the vertical working line. Choose the one that best suits your situation, then make a dry run with loose tiles or your tile stick to check the layout for inconvenient cuts. Sometimes a minor adjustment in the position of the vertical line can make your work easier. When you are satisfied, mark the vertical lines on both end walls. If your situation is unusual, consult your tile dealer, distributor, or manufacturer.

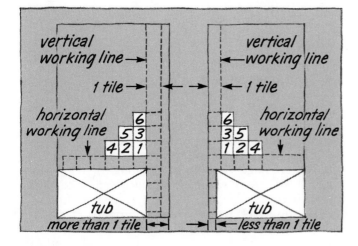

vertical working line →

1 tile →

horizontal working line

6
5 3
4 2 1

vertical working line →

6
3 5
1 2 4

1 tile

horizontal working line

tub

tub

more than 1 tile →

less than 1 tile →

If you established your horizontal working line from the low point of the tub, nail battens temporarily to the wall with the top edges on the horizontal working line. Wood strips, 1" by 2" or 1" by 3", will do the job. Not only do the battens align your tiles, but they prevent them from slipping until the adhesive sets. At that time you can remove the battens and cut and set the bottom row of tiles.

You can also use this method if you're working from the high point of the tub. However, it works almost as well to set the tiles in the bottom row first, carefully aligning their tops with the horizontal line. Hold the tiles in position with shims between their bottoms and the tub lip. The positions of any flush-mounted or recessed accessories, such as soap dishes and towel bars, should be marked at this time. If your accessories were made by the same manufacturer as your tiles, the spaces needed will usually be the same as one or two tiles. As you set the tiles, just omit tiles wherever the accessories are to go. Some recessed soap dishes require openings in the backing. If yours is that type, cut the hole now.

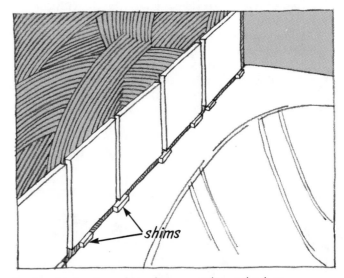

shims

For level tub, *place shims between tiles and tub to align tile tops with horizontal working line.*

Some final hints. Before you go on to the next step and spread the adhesive, you might want to mark another horizontal line where your tile will end. This will guide you as you apply the adhesive so you won't spread more than necessary. Of course, if you intend to tile all the way to the ceiling, you won't need to do this. With your tile stick, measure up along each vertical working line, from the horizontal working line to the top of the last tile course. You should have at least one course above the shower head. Once you've marked the points on the vertical working lines, extend a horizontal line through them around the tub.

Laying the Tile

Now, at last, you are ready to start laying tiles. When laying square or rectangular tiles, you have a choice of two bonds (patterns). The bottom one illustrated on page 53, known as jack-on-jack, has all its joints aligned. The top one is called a running bond; here the joints are staggered. With the latter bond you may have to cut more tiles.

The method for setting the more common jack-on-jack bond is described below. To set the running bond, place the middle of the first tile on your vertical working line. Then set the succeeding tiles in the sequence illustrated on page 53.

Tiling the back wall. Spread your adhesive on the back wall as described on page 46. Be sure to leave blank spaces in the proper locations for later installation of accessories.

Setting the first tile. If you nailed a batten to the wall, set the first tile at the intersection of the vertical guideline and the batten (see page 53, top). Use a slight twisting motion, but don't slide the tile —this will push the adhesive up on the edge of the tile, preventing a tight fit with the adjoining tile when it is laid. Make sure that the tile is tight against the batten with one edge aligned exactly with the vertical line.

When working without a batten, you still set the first tile at the intersection of the two working lines, but the *top* edge is aligned with the horizontal working line. Stick several wood shims between the tub lip and the bottom of the tile to keep it from sliding. Press firmly to bed the tile in the bond coat.

Building the pyramid. Now set a tile on each side of the first tile, with the bottoms on the batten and the adjoining spacing lugs tight against each other. Use a slight twisting motion as you put each one in place. If your tiles have no lugs, you can use finishing nails as spacers (see page 53), or cord (see page 46).

Set the next tile—the fourth—in the same fashion, exactly above the first one, with one edge on the vertical working line. Continue setting tiles in the sequence shown on page 53, using the twisting motion and adding spacers if they are needed. As the pyramid develops in a step pattern, make sure that the corners are aligned. Painstaking attention to detail now will result in a professional-looking job.

As you reach the ends of each row, measure, mark, and cut the end tiles as needed (see "Marking and Cutting Ceramic Tiles," page 47). Set the cut pieces in place with a slight twist.

Even though you push the tiles firmly into place, they may not be level with each other. After you've set a few tiles, beat them in by tapping with a hammer on a block of wood as you slide it across the tiles.

Finishing the top. If you are tiling only part way up the wall, the last course or row of tiles should be bullnose tiles. These have one edge rounded and glazed; they may be full-size or half-size tiles (sometimes known as caps).

If you're tiling all the way to the ceiling, you'll probably have to cut the last course to fit. Measure, mark, and cut these tiles and set them as you go along.

After setting the last tile, check your workmanship. Are all the joints aligned? If not, wiggle the offending tiles into position. If any tiles project above their neighbors, beat them in again with the hammer and block of wood. Clean any adhesive from the face of the tile and from the joints if filled with adhesive.

Tiling the end walls. Now that you've finished the back wall, the end walls are next. Spread adhesive on the wall opposite the shower head; it is the easier of the two.

If you're laying tile in a running bond, you may want to adjust your starting point. Corner tiles of equal width on the adjoining walls can result in a more pleasing appearance. Check by making a dry run. In any event, stagger alternate rows by half the width of a tile, as you did on the back wall.

Rotate the first tile slightly as you set it in place at the intersection of the vertical working line and the batten. Make sure that the tile is tight against the batten and that one edge is exactly on the vertical line.

If you are working without a batten, align the top edge of the tile with the horizontal working line and insert shims between the tile's bottom edge and the tub lip to prevent sliding.

Place the second and third tiles as shown in drawing on page 55, bottom, aligning them with the first. Make sure they're tight against each other, and don't forget the spacers if your tiles have no lugs.

Continue setting tiles, maintaining the step pattern as you work toward the corner. Beat the tiles in as you go, and check alignment frequently.

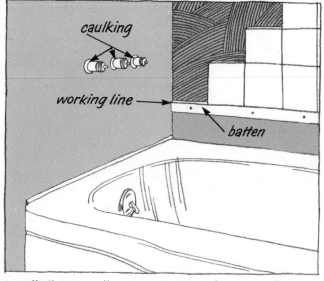

Install tiles *on wall in step, or pyramid pattern. After adhesive dries, remove batten and place tiles in remaining space.*

In the corner, cut tiles to fit as needed. If you're not tiling to the ceiling, set the top course with bullnose tiles.

Next, spread your adhesive on the other wall and lay the tiles in a similar manner. This wall requires more effort, since you must cut tiles to fit around the faucets and shower head (see below and "Marking and Cutting Ceramic Tiles," page 47).

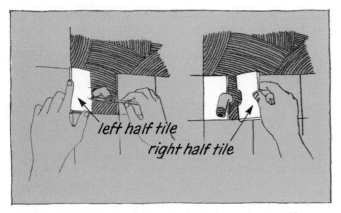

Mark *pipe center on tile's top edge and cut in two. Then mark pipe on cut edge of each piece (left). Remove excess with nippers and set pieces in place (right).*

While waiting for the adhesive to set, check your work and realign any tiles that need it. Carefully clean off any adhesive from the faces of the tile and clean out the joints if needed.

After the adhesive has set, carefully remove the battens. Spread adhesive between the bottom of the tile and the tub lip. Set tiles in the vacant space, cutting them to fit if necessary. When cutting, maintain a ⅛″ gap between tiles and tub. Don't forget to beat these tiles after they're set.

Now set the legs—the tiles in front of the tub on either side—and the columns of tiles above them. Depending on your situation, these may be bullnose tiles, field tiles, or a combination of the two.

If your accessories (such as towel bars and the soap dish) are also ceramic, and if they're flush-

Install accessories, *such as soap dish, last. Apply adhesive either to wall or to back of accessory.*

mounted or recessed, now is the time to set them. A word on safety: grab bars should be securely fastened through both tile and backing to the studs. Metal accessories shouldn't be set until you've grouted the joints. If your adhesive is mastic, use the floor type for the accessories—it dries faster.

Finishing Up

While waiting for the adhesive to dry, clean excess adhesive from the tile faces and the joints. Grout the joints as described in "Applying Grouts," page 62.

With a good bathtub caulk, seal the opening between the bottom of the tiles and the tub. Use

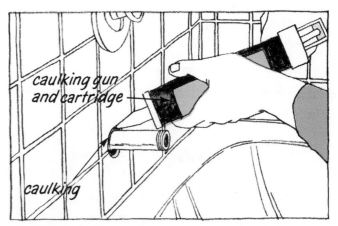

Filling gap *between tile and tub or shower with caulk seals backing and adhesive from water.*

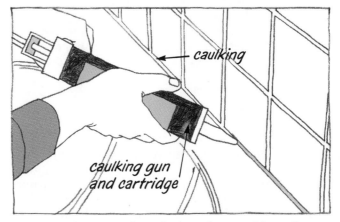

Thoroughly seal *openings between pipes and tile with good-quality bathtub caulk.*

the same compound for the openings between the tiles and the faucets and shower head. If you are using surface-mounted accessories, mark and drill the holes and fasten the accessories with toggle bolts or other type of anchor. Metal recessed soap dishes require a bead of caulking applied behind the flange. Wipe off any that squeezes out when you mount the dish.

After the grout has dried and you have sealed it (see page 63), your tub is ready to use.

Tiling a Shower

Installing tile in a shower is probably the most difficult basic tiling project for the do-it-yourselfer. The wet, steamy environment demands careful attention to selection and installation of the backing, choice of adhesive, and installation of the tile. Then the joints must be properly grouted and other openings completely sealed. The restricted working space in many showers adds to the difficulty.

Traditionally the receptor—the bottom of the shower—is constructed on the job with cement mortar, a waterproof membrane, and ceramic tile. For a watertight job, this is best left to a professional. However, a variety of prefabricated receptors are available for the do-it-yourselfer building a shower. Check with a plumbing supply house.

Tiling a shower is similar to tiling a tub enclosure, so the instructions beginning on page 54 will help you. The receptor has the same relationship to the tile as a tub does.

Preparing the surface. Prepare the existing surface or install new backing if needed. If you're installing new backing, refer to the illustration below showing the construction where tub and wall meet. A word of caution: water-resistant gypsum board is not recommended for use on ceilings. Use regular gypsum board and seal it well.

Laying out the job. As with a tub enclosure, mark the working lines first on the back wall, then the sides. If your shower walls partially enclose the front, use the back corners as your vertical working lines if the back wall is plumb. Any cut tiles will be hidden in the front corners.

Setting the tile. Spread adhesive on the back wall and set the tiles as described in "Tiling a Tub

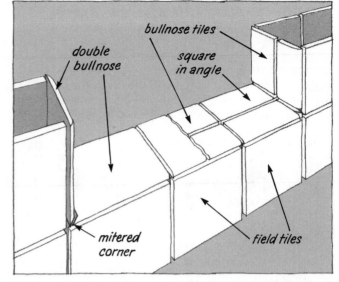

Two ways to trim a shower opening: Right half shows opening trimmed with bullnose caps; left half has double bullnose tiles. Slope bottom of opening slightly toward inside of shower.

Enclosure," page 54. When the back is complete, do the sides of the shower. Tile work on the front of an enclosed shower is done last. Set any ceramic accessories.

Many professionally built showers have tiled ceilings. If you want to tile yours, do it before the walls. Since gravity is always at work, you may need some means to hold the tile in position until the adhesive sets. Pieces of plywood wedged against the ceiling with 2 by 4s will work.

Grouting and finishing up. After the adhesive is dry, carefully grout all the joints between the tiles (see page 62). Use a good bathtub caulk to seal the joints between receptor and tile and between tile and faucet handles and shower head. After the grout has dried, apply a sealer as described on page 63.

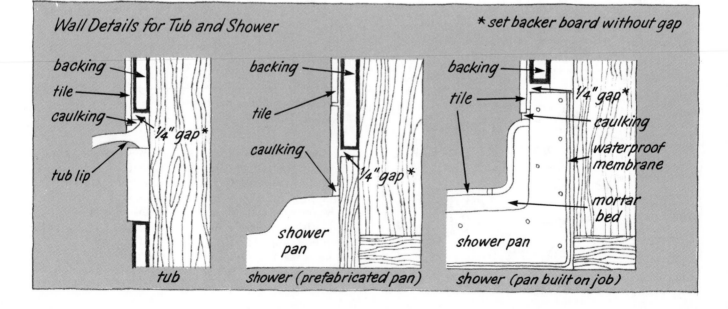

Tiling Sinks and Counter Tops

Installing ceramic tile on a counter top or similar surface is a good do-it-yourself project for the beginner. A sink top in the bathroom or kitchen, a new top for a bar or vanity, an elegant buffet in the dining room, or open storage shelves in the kitchen—all are within your capabilities as a tile setter.

The instructions that follow will guide you as you tile a sink top. You can adapt them easily to other projects. If you're tiling a counter top or buffet, just ignore the portion about sinks. If you want to tile storage shelves, you can forget both sinks and backsplashes.

Choose the edge trim. Before you start, you must decide how you will trim the counter edge. The usual methods are illustrated below; your choice will depend on the availability of trim pieces in your pattern as well as on personal preference. So too with the sink—it may be set on top of the tile, mounted flush, or set in and finished with quarter-round tile trim. Be sure to apply caulking as shown between the sink and backing or tile.

Preparing the Surface

You can apply new tiles right over existing ceramic tile or laminated plastic counters. Refer to the section on existing backings, page 44, for information on preparing these surfaces. That section also tells you how to prepare the wall behind for tiling as a backsplash.

If you installed new cabinets or removed the old counter top, you'll be installing a new backing. The illustrations below give structural details. Be sure the backing is fastened tightly to the cabinets and walls with nails or screws. Make sure to leave enough clearance between the edge trim and appliances, such as a dishwasher, that pull out.

As a material for the new backing, there are two choices: ¾"-thick exterior plywood or backer board.

Plywood is by far the most common backing for ceramic tile counter tops. Exterior grade is preferred, as the waterproof glue used in its construction gives added protection against moisture.

Since the key to a successful tile job is a good base, support the plywood so it is rigid. If the width of the top is 24" or less, a cross-brace every 36" in addition to the supports at front and back is adequate. Design and build any overhangs or cantilevered sections so they are strong and rigid.

With a plywood backing, you may use either mastic or epoxy adhesives. Mastic is commonly used; if this is your choice, Type I will give you greater water resistance. For water protection and better adherence, most manufacturers recommend sealing the face and edges of the plywood with a sealer/bonderizer (see page 45).

Epoxy adhesive gives more protection against water; but it is more difficult to work with. If you use epoxy, leave a gap of ¼" between plywood panels. Nail a wood batten beneath each gap to prevent the epoxy from dripping through.

Backer board, a new product, has not yet been widely used on counter tops. It has many of the attributes of a mortar bed (see page 43), so you might consider using it as a backing for counter tops subject to moisture. Because backer board lacks sufficient strength of its own, nail and glue it to ¾" plywood as described under "New Backings," page 43. With backer board, use either dry-set or latex–Portland cement mortar (see page 39).

Planning the Layout

On the front edge of the backing, locate and mark the point where the center of the sink will be. If your counter top won't have a sink, then mark the midpoint of the top. The point you mark will be the starting point for your tile work.

(Continued on next page)

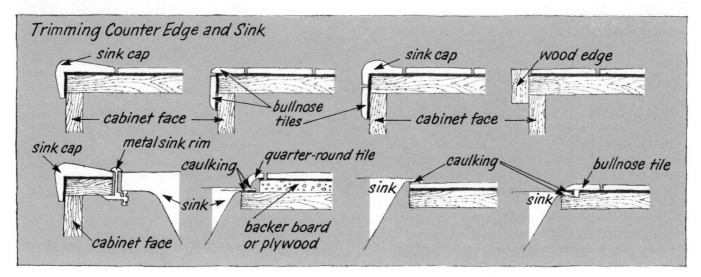

Trimming Counter Edge and Sink

. . . Continued from page 59

Next, lay the edge tiles out loose on the counter top. Start with a sink cap or other edge trim, aligning one of its edges with the center mark. Use spacers or a tile stick to establish the grout joints. If necessary, adjust the first tile's position to eliminate narrow cuts. Carefully position the rest of the tiles on the counter and make whatever adjustments you can to eliminate strange cuts or difficult fits. By resolving these before you start setting the tiles, you will improve the look of the finished job. You can mark and cut the tiles now or wait until you are ready to set them. Be sure to allow for the cove if you're using one for the backsplash.

After arriving at the optimum layout, you may feel that you'll have difficulty duplicating it when you set the tiles. If this is the case, either mark the locations of key tiles on the backing or set the edge trim before you remove the other tiles (see "Setting the Tile," below). Then you can mark your reference points on the edge trim.

Setting the Tile

In this project you set the trim pieces first, before you spread the adhesive for the field tiles.

Place the sink caps first. If your tile has no lugs, use spacers to maintain the grout joints. (See page 46). Continue until all the sink caps are set.

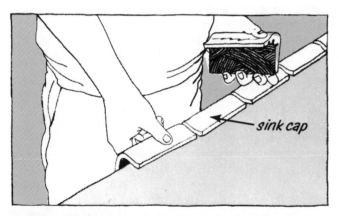

Set edge tiles *in place after buttering backs with adhesive.*

If your edge trim consists of two pieces (see page 59) instead of the one-piece sink cap, set the vertical piece on the front of the counter first.

After all the sink caps or other edge trim pieces are set, set the back cove against the wall. (Disregard this paragraph if you're not using cove tiles.) Butter the back of each tile and press into place with a slight twisting motion. Be sure to line tiles up with your reference marks for the field tiles.

Unless the sink is mounted flush or on top of the tile, lay the sink trim next. Be sure to caulk between the sink and the backing before setting the sink trim. Butter each trim piece as you set it.

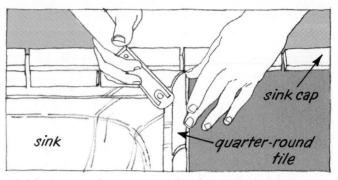

Finish *corners of quarter-round sink trim with round in-angle or by mitering as shown.*

If you're using quarter-round tiles, you can either miter the corners or use the quarter-round corner trim available in some patterns.

After all the trim pieces are in position, spread the adhesive over a section of counter (see directions on page 46). Don't spread more than you can cover with the tile during the open time. If you are using epoxy, be sure to fill the ¼" gaps between plywood sheets with the adhesive.

Now lay the field tiles, working from the front to the back and cutting back pieces to fit as necessary. If you're not using a back cove, the tiles should run to the wall. Work from the sink toward the ends to avoid a cut edge at the sink. If your project has no sink, start laying the field tiles from the center of the counter and work toward both ends. Be sure to use spacers if the tiles don't have lugs (see page 46); check frequently with your square.

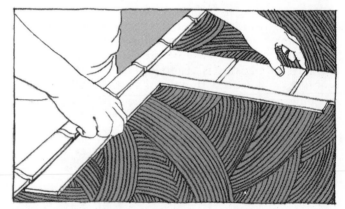

Start *installing field tiles by setting column of tiles. Use square to keep tiles perpendicular to edge trim.*

Beat in the tiles to level the faces as you lay them. Slide a piece of plywood, about 1' square, over the tiles while tapping it with a hammer.

Now set the backsplash. If you used a cove, continue setting the tiles on the wall to the height desired after covering the area with adhesive. Unless you're tiling up to an overhead cabinet or window sill, use bullnose tiles for the last row. If you didn't use cove tiles, start the backsplash with regular field tiles. Space these above the

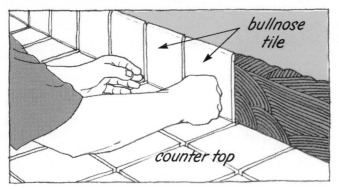

Align joints *of backsplash tiles with joints on counter top. Leave width of one grout joint between counter tiles and bottom of backsplash tiles.*

When backsplash *is higher than one course, you may have to fit tiles around electrical outlets. Either cut hole in tile or cut tile in two and nibble out hole.*

counter tiles the width of a grout joint.

You may run into situations we haven't covered here. If the wall behind the counter contains electrical outlets or switches, you can either stop the backsplash short of them or cut the tile and reset them as described on page 53. A window sill behind a sink can be finished with bullnose tiles or you can run the tile up to the sill. Some faucets are mounted on the tile behind the sink. If this is

your situation, mark and cut the tiles as described on page 47.

Applying Grout

Clean all adhesive from the tile face and the grout joints. After the adhesive has dried for the prescribed time, grout the tiles as described on page 62. When the grout is thoroughly dry, be sure to seal it (see "Caring for Ceramic Tile," page 63).

Some Quick and Simple Projects

If you've never installed ceramic tile, you may want to begin with a small project that will test your skills and give you quick results. Any of the following projects will add a colorful accent, and since these installations cover small areas, you can use some of the more expensive decorative tiles without straining the budget.

Whether you're tiling a window sill or an entire floor, the basic procedures are the same. Be sure to read the section "Preparing the Surface" (see page 42), as well as the information on adhesives and grouts (see pages 39 and 40). To learn the techniques of setting, cutting, and finishing tile, see "How to Install Ceramic Tile" (page 46).

Stair treads and risers. Some manufacturers offer a special tile known as step nosing for use on treads. If these aren't available, you can use bullnose tiles set with the rounded edges toward the front of the step. A special trim piece called down-corner (see page 35) is ideal for finishing the corners of exposed treads. Use the same installation procedure you would for other

horizontal surfaces such as floors or counters (see pages 48 and 59).

Cover stair risers with field tiles, using the same method you would to tile a wall (see page 51). The top edges of the riser tiles will be covered by the tread nosing.

If you plan to tile both the treads and the risers, do the risers first.

Window sills. Special tiles called window sills are available from some tile makers. Or you can use bullnose tiles; set them with the rounded edges to the front. If the wall below the window is also tiled, the tiles on the sill should overlap the top edges of the wall tiles.

Fireplaces. Tiling the face of a fireplace is similar to installing tile on a wall (see page 51). You can also install a row of tiles around the inside of the fireplace. Depending on the design of your fireplace, you can use bullnose, double bullnose, or regular field tiles for either job.

If the face of the fireplace is masonry, install the tile with cement-based adhesive. On nonmasonry surfaces, use mastic to set the tiles; be sure to let the mastic dry thoroughly—at least 24 hours—before

using the fireplace. Tiles installed anywhere inside the fireplace, where they will be directly exposed to the flames, should always be set with cement-based adhesives.

You can tile the hearth just as you would tile a floor (see page 48). Again, use cement-based adhesives.

Decorative inserts and borders. To add a decorative border of tiles around a door or window, you can fasten tiles directly to the wall with mastic. Another way is to inset the tiles flush with the face of the wall.

To inset tiles in a wall of gypsum board, cut out openings the same size as the tiles. Apply a bead of glue toward the edges of a couple of pieces of wallboard or plywood; slip them at an angle through the opening and fasten against the back side of the wall, closing the opening as much as possible. This forms a recessed surface for the tiles.

For plaster walls, chip out recesses to a depth equal to the thickness of the tiles and set the tiles with a cement-based adhesive. For both gypsum board and plaster walls, fill the gaps around the edges of the tiles with patching plaster.

Final Touches...from Grouting to Care

Now you can turn to the finishing touches that will complete your tile project. The first one is applying grout to fill joints, bond tiles together, and add visual appeal. Next comes care—applying a sealer or wax to preserve tile and grout.

Applying Grouts

All grouts except silicone rubber grouts are applied in the same basic way: fill the joints, remove the excess, clean the tile, and allow to cure. Silicone grouts are applied directly to the joints from tube or cartridge.

Allow the adhesive to set properly before applying the grout. This takes 48 hours with tiles set in cement mortars, 24 hours with mastics, and 16 hours with epoxy adhesives.

While the adhesive is drying, remove any spacers used to position the tiles and clean the tile surface so it is completely free of adhesive. If the joints are too shallow to hold grout because of adhesive, clean them out.

To prevent some cement-based grouts from drying prematurely, wash white-bodied and soft red-bodied tiles before grouting. These porous bodies draw liquid from the grout, making it weak after curing. Damp-curing of cement-based grouts, by covering with plastic for 24 hours, is often recommended.

With a cement-based grout, an additive may make the grout easier to work and extend its working life. Follow the manufacturer's instructions both for mixing the grout and using additives, if these are not already in the grout. If you want colored grout, add the color now. Properly mixed cement grouts have the consistency of pancake batter—stiff for mosaics, loose for white-bodied tiles, and soupy for red-bodied tiles. Epoxy grouts are used exactly as mixed according to the manufacturer's directions.

Although you can apply grout with only your fingers and a large sponge, you will find the job much easier if you use a rubber-faced float or a squeegee. You should also have an old toothbrush to help work grout into joints and finish off narrow joints between wall or counter tiles. Keep a supply of clear water and soft cloths available for cleaning. Many grouts can irritate the skin, so be sure to wear gloves.

Here are the steps in applying grout:

1) Apply grout to the surface of the tile, spreading it with the float or squeegee and forcing it into the joints. Be sure that the joints are completely filled, with no voids or air pockets.

2) Scrape off the excess grout, working diagonally across the tiles with your float or squeegee.

3) Soak your sponge in clear water and wring it out. Wipe the tiles, removing any remaining grout. Rinse and wring out the sponge frequently until the joints are smooth and level with the tiles. When the tiles are as clean as you can get them with the sponge, let the grout dry until a haze appears over the surface.

4) After the remaining grout on the tiles has dried to a haze (about 30 minutes), polish it off with a soft cloth. Use the end of a toothbrush handle to tool the joints and clean the intersections.

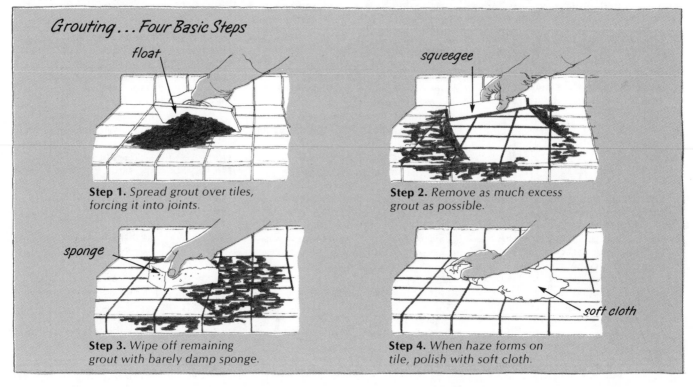

Grouting... Four Basic Steps

float

squeegee

Step 1. *Spread grout over tiles, forcing it into joints.*

Step 2. *Remove as much excess grout as possible.*

sponge

soft cloth

Step 3. *Wipe off remaining grout with barely damp sponge.*

Step 4. *When haze forms on tile, polish with soft cloth.*

Caring for Ceramic Tile

Once you've installed your tile, and had a chance to stand back and admire your work, you'll want to consider how to keep the tile looking like new for years to come. Installations with unglazed tile and those with cement-based grouts need the initial protection of a grout and tile sealer. This product is available from most tile dealers. Beyond that, routine cleaning and annual reapplication of sealer are all that's required to maintain the tile's original beauty. Glazed tiles and epoxy-based or silicone-based grouts need not be sealed, though they too should be cleaned regularly.

Sealing Tile and Grout

Most sealers use silicone or lacquer as a base. *Silicone-based sealers* are usually used in and around showers, bathtubs, and other wet areas. They wipe off glazed tile surfaces easily, while penetrating the cement-based grout between the tiles. *Lacquer-based sealers* break down in wet areas, but they penetrate unglazed tile pores better than the silicone sealers. You can get lacquer-based sealers in gloss and nongloss finishes. The gloss finish may make tiles slippery, so test the sealer before you apply it to floors.

Follow manufacturer's instructions for applying tile and grout sealers. On new tile installations, wait at least 2 weeks before applying the sealer, to give the grout a chance to cure completely. Both tiles and grout should be completely dry. Take extra care not to apply too much sealer, and wipe off any excess to prevent the tile from discoloring.

Tile Waxes

After they're sealed, unglazed tile floors may be waxed and buffed for additional beauty and protection. Tile waxes should be used in dry areas only, because water will discolor them.

After cleaning the surface, apply the wax according to label directions, then buff with a floor polisher. A properly applied wax will last several years, requiring only an occasional buffing. Too much wax left on the tile's surface, however, turns yellow even when buffed. If this happens, you can strip off the old wax by scrubbing with hot water and detergent or with a commercial wax stripper.

Cleaning Tips

Ceramic tile is among the easiest surfaces to keep clean. Routine cleaning requires only washing with hot water and a mild detergent or all-purpose household cleaner. To prevent stains, wipe up spills as soon as they happen.

After washing the tile, rinse it thoroughly to remove detergent film, then dry it by polishing with a soft, dry cloth. For stubborn dirt, scrub tiles with a white cleansing powder (colored powders may tint the grout) or a concentrated solution of all-purpose cleaner. You might also try a commercial tile cleaner, available from your tile dealer or in

Working with Panels and Mosaics

Panels of wall tile (see page 35) and sheets of mosaic are similar—in both, a group of tiles are held together mechanically to simplify the installation. The panels are pregrouted, but the mosaic sheets must be grouted after they are laid.

The basic installation method is the same as that for individual tiles. But, instead of handling a single tile at a time, you have a sheet of tiles to work with.

The requirements for surface preparation and backings are the same, and you must lay out working lines with panels and sheets as with single tiles.

Sheets and panels are much faster to install than single tiles, so you will find that you can cover larger areas with adhesive. Tiles in a panel are held firmly in position by the grout, but those in a mosaic sheet are not. You may have to adjust the positions of some tiles in the sheet after laying. Mosaic sheets held together by a thread mesh are especially likely to need adjustments. Check mosaics for alignment before the adhesive sets.

Grouting the pregrouted panels takes little time. Using a caulking gun, you grout only the joints between panels. Grouting of mosaics is the same as for individual tiles.

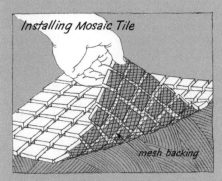
Mosaic tiles *come mounted in sheets.*

Pregrouted *tile panels save time.*

hardware stores. Always read the directions and precautions on the label before using. Some tile cleaners have harsh acids that will etch glazed tiles if left on the surface too long—use them sparingly. **Never mix cleaners containing acid or ammonia with chlorine bleach. The chemical reaction releases the chlorine as a poisonous gas.**

On floors, use a broom or dust mop to remove loose dirt and a damp mop for cleaning. For other surfaces (walls, counter tops, and so on) use a sponge or cloth to apply the cleaning solution. For rough scrubbing, use a stiff-bristled scrub brush or nylon scrubbing pad. Avoid using steel wool pads on ceramic tile—they may cause rust stains.

In addition to routine cleaning, you can keep grout looking new by scrubbing it occasionally with a toothbrush and household bleach or tile cleaner. If your grout is colored, test these cleaners in an unobtrusive place before you use them. It's hard to predict how the chemicals will react with the pigment in the grout.

If you have hard water, spots and deposits may build up on tiles that are in shower enclosures, on sink counters, and in other wet areas. You can help prevent such buildups by keeping the tile surfaces dry. Use a squeegee to wipe water off the tiles after showering or doing dishes. To remove water deposits and soap film from the tile, apply household ammonia or a one-to-one mixture of vinegar and water, rinse thoroughly, and dry.

Removing Stains from Tile

Even the hardest tile surface may pick up a stain or two. Tile, grout, and stains all come in so many kinds that no simple rules for stain removal can be given. The chart below covers the most common and troublesome stains. If a stain remains after one try, try again. If the cleaner you're using seems too weak, make it more concentrated. In most cases, heating a solution will cause it to work faster.

Replacing Grout

If grout is cracked, badly worn, or permanently stained, you can easily replace it. Scrape the old grout from the joints with a lever-type can opener; then scrub the joint surfaces clean with scouring powder or tile cleaner. Rinse the surface well. Apply the grout, following the instructions on page 62 or directions on the package. Most hardware stores sell grout in small quantities for replacement purposes.

What to Do When Tiles Get Stained

Stain	Cleaner	Method
Ink, blood, coffee, mustard, fruit juice	Household bleach	Leave bleach on surface for several minutes, then rinse off. (Test before using on colored grout.)
Motor oil or grease (on quarry or patio tile)	Fluid mixture of plaster of Paris and water (to draw stain out)	Brush over the surface in a thin coat. Let dry and harden for 12 to 24 hours. Remove with stiff brush. Apply again if needed.
Vegetable oil or grease (on quarry or patio tile)	Detergent, sodium carbonate, sodium hydroxide	If detergent doesn't work, scrub surface with 10% sodium carbonate (washing soda) solution in water. Mop with 5% sodium hydroxide (caustic soda) for faster action.
Marks from steel tools, rust stains, stubborn hard water deposits, surface stains on grout (with Portland cement base), efflorescence	Scouring powder. If stain remains, commercial tile cleaner	Scrub on scouring powder with damp rag; let stand. Rinse well. If using tile cleaner, follow label directions.
Wet paper carton stains	Household bleach, emery cloth (for unglazed tile)	Same as for ink and blood, but finish with fine emery cloth.
Paint (new stain)	Commercial paint remover	Apply paint remover. Let it stand (follow label directions), then remove paint with scraper and bristle brush (glazed tile) or wire brush (unglazed tile).
Paint (old stain), dried plaster	Razor blade held almost flat	Scrape loose. Work carefully. Paint remover may help.

Some Other Choices in Tile Materials

In addition to the popular tiles—ceramic, wood, and resilient—covered in this book, you'll also find tiles made from other materials. Perhaps one of the kinds discussed below will be just right for your remodeling job.

Carpet tiles are easily installed over most smooth floor surfaces. Most commonly available in 12″ squares, these tiles have a built-in foam padding. Carpet tiles come in three kinds: those with a self-stick backing; those with a nonskid rubber backing that requires no adhesive; and those laid with an adhesive in the same way as resilient tiles. Carpet tiles are easy to replace if they become worn or damaged.

Mirror tiles, usually 12″ square, come with a wide variety of surface designs. Applied to a wall, they add depth and light to any room. They are affixed to a surface with double-faced mounting tape.

Marble tiles, precut to various sizes, may be used in the same ways as ceramic tile. Long considered a hallmark of opulence, marble tiles cost about the same as high-quality ceramic tiles or hardwood flooring. Installation is similar to that of ceramic tile.

Slate tiles are bluish black, green, or maroon in color, with either a smooth or—more often—a textured surface. Slate floors are durable and restful to the eyes.

Terrazzo tile is made by setting chips of marble or onyx in concrete and polishing the surface. Though commonly made in large slabs, terrazzo is also available in 12″ tiles that can be installed by the homeowner.

Polyester tiles (sometimes called epoxy tiles) consist of pulverized stone bonded in polyester or other plastic. These extremely durable tiles are set like ceramic tile.

Metal tiles of copper, stainless steel, or aluminum harmonize well with kitchen appliances. Metal tiles are easy to clean and won't chip or crack. They give kitchens and bathrooms a space-age look.

Plastic tiles can replace ceramic tiles in low-wear, high-moisture situations such as tub and shower enclosures and sink backsplashes. They cost about one-fifth as much as their ceramic equivalents.

Marble *is just one of many other kinds of tiling materials available; installation is similar to ceramic tile. Tile by Bufalini Marble Corporation.*

RESILIENT TILE

. . . attractive, economical, easy to maintain

Traditional *or contemporary, simulated brick or marble, textured or smooth,*
resilient tile offers a wide variety of look-alikes as well as original designs.

Does a new floor with the appearance of Italian marble or Spanish tile appeal to you? How about one with a wild, colorful graphic design of your own creation? From traditional to contemporary, today's resilient tiles offer a vast range of colors, textures, and patterns to whet your creative appetite. Vinyl-asbestos and solid vinyl tiles not only simulate almost every known flooring material but also offer many designs unique to resilient tile. Even real cork or a fine hardwood sealed in vinyl can grace your home.

Compared to most other floors, resilient tile is economical and easy to install and care for. Installation requires only a little skill and a few basic tools.

Resilient tiles are by no means restricted to the floor. They're becoming a popular wall covering material, too. You can use any of the standard floor tiles or ones designed especially for walls. See page 72 for a discussion of resilient tile on walls.

Making Your Choice

When you shop for resilient tile, you'll find an ample selection of designs, colors, and textures. Resilient tiles vary in composition; consider the qualities of each kind before you choose.

Kinds Available

The composition of a resilient tile—the stuff it's made of—is just as important as its visual appearance. The tile you choose should be durable, comfortable underfoot, and easy to install and maintain. Keep this in mind when you make your selection from the resilient tiles discussed below:

Asphalt tile. The forerunner of modern resilient tiles, asphalt tile is still available for replacement purposes, though it's increasingly hard to find. Less durable than vinyl-asbestos and solid vinyl tiles and available in fewer patterns and colors, asphalt tile is rarely installed in homes today.

Vinyl-asbestos tile. The most popular resilient tile available today, vinyl-asbestos offers the widest selection of colors, patterns, and textures.

Vinyl-asbestos tile has excellent resistance to moisture, dirt, wear, and indentation. In addition,

many vinyl-asbestos tiles have either one or both of the following features:

• a self-stick back surface for easy installation. You simply peel off the paper backing, press the tile in place, and walk on it.

• a bonded "no-wax" urethane surface that retains its shine without waxing. The easy-to-clean surface can be polished occasionally with a special polish available from the tile manufacturer.

Solid vinyl tiles. These popular tiles have the same advantages as vinyl-asbestos, including the features mentioned above. Though more expensive than vinyl-asbestos tiles, solid vinyl tiles offer brighter color and gloss. Their durable, nonporous surfaces make them easier to care for.

Variations. Though vinyl-asbestos and solid vinyl tiles simulate many flooring materials, you may prefer the "real thing." Cork tile, a naturally resilient material, is an excellent choice where you want a soft, warm, quiet floor surface. Today's cork tile comes with a tough vinyl coating to give it the durability and easy maintenance of vinyl-asbestos and solid vinyl surfaces.

Some variations of vinyl-asbestos and solid vinyl tiles involve materials such as fabric, hardwood veneers, or marble chips. These materials are suspended in solid vinyl or laminated between a base and a tough vinyl wearing surface. Resilient tiles designed especially for walls include simulated brick, wood shake, and ceramic designs. You can even buy a special grout to give simulated ceramic and brick designs a more realistic look.

Other Considerations

Once you've decided on a kind of resilient tile, you'll want to choose a design, color, and texture to complement your room decor. Here are a few points to consider while making your choice:

• Textured tiles are embossed with a grained, pitted, or fissured surface. Embossing helps to hide seams, wear marks, and indentations left by furniture. However, you must be careful not to let wax or polish build up in the recesses.

• Solid colors, especially black and white, tend to show dirt more than marbled or patterned tiles. An embossed tile with a strong, variegated pattern is

Feature strips *set off plain tile designs.*

Create *floor design on graph paper with colored pencils.*

a good choice in a room where the floor will take a beating.

• In a large room, you can break up the expanse of a continuous pattern with feature strips, shown above. Feature strips are long vinyl or vinyl-asbestos strips of various widths, used as accents or borders in tile designs. Be sure to choose strips of the same material and thickness as the tile you're using.

• For a professional-looking job, you can replace the existing base molding with vinyl or rubber cove base, available from your tile dealer. Cove base for resilient floors comes in various sizes and colors. Ask your tile dealer for instructions on installing cove base.

How Much Will You Need?

Resilient tiles come in two standard sizes, 9" square and 12" square. Other sizes and shapes are available, but they must usually be ordered specially.

To find the amount of tile you need, first find the area of the floor. Get this by multiplying the overall length of the room by its width, both in feet. Deduct the area of any protrusions in the room, such as a kitchen counter or a bathtub. For a room with an odd shape, such as an L-shaped room, divide the floor area into rectangles. Then measure each and add the areas together. Once you've found the area, add 8 percent so you'll have extra tiles for cutting and waste.

Resilient tile comes in boxes that contain 45 square feet. To find the number of boxes you need, divide the overall floor area (including 8 percent extra) by 45. Buy a few extra tiles and save them to replace ones that become damaged. Unless tiles must be ordered specially, most tile dealers will break a box to sell you the exact number of tiles you want. Check boxes for color consistency.

If you're designing a tile floor using more than one color or pattern, you can estimate how many

tiles of each kind you'll need by drawing your design on graph paper with colored pencils, as shown above.

When you go to buy the tile, pick up adhesive (unless you're using self-stick tiles) and, if necessary, the proper notched trowel to spread it. Your tile dealer can help you choose these.

Before you go, evaluate the surface you'll be laying the tile on. Refer to the section on preparing the surface, on the facing page, to determine if you'll need additional tools and materials for preliminary work.

Tools You'll Need

You may already have most of the tools needed to install resilient tile. To measure and mark the working lines, you'll need a folding rule or steel tape, square, pencil, and chalk line. If you'll be marking working lines on walls, you'll also need a level.

To cut the tiles, use a utility knife or linoleum knife. Solid vinyl tiles, as well as thin vinyl-asbestos tiles that have been heated, can be cut with a pair of heavy scissors (see page 72 for information on cutting tiles). To spread the adhesive, you'll need a brush, paint roller, or notched trowel—whichever is specified by the tile or adhesive manufacturer. If you're installing solid vinyl tiles, you'll need a rolling pin to bed the tiles into the adhesive.

How to Install Resilient Tile

Ease of installation makes resilient tile popular with do-it-yourselfers. The key to a professional-looking job is proper planning and preparation. First, you must have a suitable subfloor on which to lay the tile. Next, you must measure accurately so the tiles will fit properly. Finally, you must fix the tiles in place so they'll adhere tightly to the subfloor.

Working carefully, follow the methods outlined in this section as well as any instructions provided with the tile you're installing.

Before you start, remove from the floor everything that isn't nailed down—and some things that are. This includes base moldings, thresholds (if any), and doors that swing into the room. If the base molding has a shoe—a thin wood strip at its lower edge—only the shoe need be removed. If you plan to put the base or shoe back after you finish tiling, pry it carefully from the wall with a wood chisel or putty knife, remove the nails, and patch the nail holes in each strip. If your plans call for replacing the wood base molding with vinyl cove base, be careful not to damage the wall as you remove the wood base.

Preparing the Surface

Resilient tile can be installed over almost any existing surface if the surface is properly prepared. Generally, the surface must be structurally sound, dry, and free from foreign matter such as grease, wax, dirt, and old finish. You can lay resilient tile over floors painted with latex if the paint is in good condition—no peeling, flaking, or chalking.

General directions for preparing common floor surfaces for resilient tile are given below. Follow these in conjunction with the directions that come with the tile you're installing.

Old resilient floors. Resilient tile can be installed over an existing resilient floor if the existing floor is smooth (not embossed or textured) and still sticks tightly to the subfloor. In addition, all existing wax and finishes must be removed before the new floor is laid. If your floor doesn't meet these requirements, you must either remove the existing flooring or cover it with a suitable underlayment recommended by the tile manufacturer. Vinyl floors laid with epoxy adhesives are difficult to remove; these are best covered with underlayment sheets (see "Double wood floors" at right). **Caution: Do not sand resilient floor coverings or backing material. These materials may contain asbestos fibers that could damage your lungs if inhaled.**

To remove resilient sheet flooring, cut it into strips with a utility knife or linoleum knife, being careful not to damage the subfloor. Peel or scrape the strips off, then scrape any excess backing off the subfloor with a wide putty knife or floor scraper. Next, fill any low spots with a trowel-on patching material recommended by the tile manufacturer.

To remove old resilient tiles, use a floor scraper as shown in the drawing above. If tiles don't come up easily, warm them to soften the adhesive; try an old iron over paper. (Heating won't help with the epoxy adhesive used with solid vinyl floors.) If you can't remove the tiles, cover them with underlayment sheets (see "Double wood floors" at right).

Wood floors. To begin with, never install resilient tile over a wood floor unless it has at least 2' of

Floor scraper *quickly removes large sections of old resilient tile or resilient sheet flooring.*

well-ventilated space between it and the ground. If your wood floor doesn't have this clearance—or if you suspect it won't, for any reason, make a suitable underlayment—consult your tile dealer or a professional flooring contractor.

Double wood floors (finish wood floor over subfloor) of boards less than 4" wide: These should be smooth and structurally sound. If necessary, renail any loose boards, then sand the floor smooth with a floor sander. (Floor sanders can be rented at tool rental shops, hardware stores, and some flooring outlets.) When using the sander, always sand along the grain of the wood.

Next, fill any cracks, low spots, or holes with wood filler or a trowel-on underlayment material recommended by the tile manufacturer. After the floor is clean and smooth, cover it with 15-pound asphalt-saturated flooring felt paper. Your tile dealer can supply you with the proper adhesive to affix the felt paper to the subfloor.

Spread the adhesive with a notched trowel, then lay the felt paper across the floor at right angles to the boards. The edges of the paper should butt against each other but not overlap.

If the floor is in poor condition or if the floorboards are 1 by 4 tongue-and-groove, prepare it as best you can, using the procedures outlined above. Instead of using felt paper, though, cover the floor with ¼" underlayment grade plywood or hardboard. Fasten with 3-penny ring-shank or 4-penny cement-coated nails spaced 3" apart along the joints and 6" apart throughout the sheet (see drawing, page 70). When installing underlayment panels, leave gaps about the thickness of a dime between them to allow for expansion of the material.

(Continued on next page)

. . . Continued from page 69

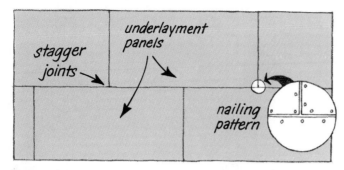

Stagger joints *on plywood underlayment panels. Offset nails around edges (see detail). Set nail heads slightly below surface; fill holes, joints with patching material.*

Single wood floors (floorboards nailed directly to joists) or double wood floors with boards over 4" wide: No matter what condition these are in, install ⅜" or ½" underlayment grade plywood. Use the same method described above for ¼" material. Use waterproof plywood in locations where the floor may be subject to excessive moisture, such as in a kitchen or bathroom. Don't use particle board, chipboard, or similar material as underlayment for resilient flooring unless it is manufactured specifically for that purpose.

In most cases, resilient tile can be installed directly over plywood or hardboard underlayments.

Concrete floors. If resilient tile is to be installed over concrete, the surface must be smooth, level, and free from dirt, grease, old finishes and sealers, and other foreign matter. Most important, the concrete floor must be perfectly dry when you install the tile and must not be subject to moisture penetration at any time. Moisture is a common problem with concrete floors poured directly on the ground ("on grade") and with concrete floors and walls below grade, as in a basement. Before you decide to install resilient tile on a concrete floor, test the floor for moisture, preferably during a wet month. In most cases the presence of moisture in the concrete indicates that you shouldn't lay resilient tile over it. (For more information, see page 45.) New concrete slabs should be allowed to cure for at least a month before a moisture test is made.

Next, remove all foreign matter from the floor—paint, sealers, oil, grease, and so on. To remove grease and oil stains, use a chemical garage floor cleaner, available from most auto supply stores. Chip or scrape off any excess concrete, globs of paint, or other foreign material. To remove paint or sealers, sand the floor to bare concrete with a floor sander and #4 or #5 open-cut sandpaper. Remove high spots by rubbing with a coarse, abrasive stone. Finish the preparation by scouring the floor with a stiff bristle brush and vacuuming up all loose material.

As a final step, fill cracks, joints, and low areas in the concrete with a latex underlayment compound as specified by the tile manufacturer. If the floor is too rough or uneven to be smoothed by the method given above, consider pouring a new slab over the old one or installing a plywood subfloor on sleepers. Unless you've had experience doing this, it's a job best left to a flooring or cement contractor.

Laying Resilient Floor Tile

When you lay resilient tile, the temperature is important. All materials as well as the room temperature must be at least 70°, not just during installation but also for at least 24 hours before and after.

Laying resilient tiles involves three basic operations: laying out the working lines, spreading the adhesive, and placing the tiles. For each operation, carefully follow the step-by-step procedures outlined below, in conjunction with any instructions that come with the tile you're using.

Laying out working lines. The drawing below shows how to mark working lines for square and diagonal tile patterns.

For a square pattern: Measure and mark the center points of two opposite walls. Disregard any offsets, alcoves, or other breaks in the walls. If you have a chalk line (available at most hardware stores), snap a line between the two points to get the first center line. If you don't have a chalk line, rub chalk on a piece of string and attach it to nails positioned at the center points; then snap the line. Follow the same procedure for the other two walls, but check the intersection of the two lines with a carpenter's square before you snap the second line to make sure it is 90°. If it isn't, adjust the chalk line.

Next, lay a row of loose tiles along one of the lines from the center point to the wall. If the space between the last tile and the wall is less than one-half tile, move the other center line one-half tile closer to the opposite wall and snap a new chalk line. Repeat this process with the other line. Doing this will insure wide border tiles around the perimeter of the room.

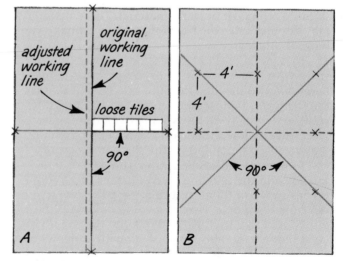

Working lines *for square tile pattern (A) and diagonal tile pattern (B) must intersect at exactly 90°.*

For a diagonal pattern: Establish center lines as you would for the square pattern, page 70, making sure they intersect at right angles. Next, mark each line at a point 4' from the center. From these points, measure out 4' in each direction perpendicular to the center lines and mark points where these lines intersect, as shown in the drawing. Snap chalk lines across these points to get diagonal working lines. If your measurements are accurate, the diagonal lines will intersect at 90° exactly at the center point. If they don't, check your measurements.

Spreading the adhesive. (If you're using self-stick tiles, you can skip this section.) Before you spread any adhesive, be sure to read the instructions on the container label thoroughly. Different adhesives require different methods of application. Some are brushed on; others are applied with a notched trowel. The proper trowel size is given on the label. The instructions will also tell you the "open time"—the amount of time you have to work with the adhesive. The open time of the adhesive, together with the speed at which you work and the size of the area to be covered, will determine which of the methods shown at right you should use for laying tiles.

Be careful not to spread the adhesive too thick. If you do, it will ooze up through the cracks between tiles. If you use too little, on the other hand, the tiles won't adhere properly.

Following application instructions on the label, begin spreading the adhesive where the working lines intersect. Spread the adhesive up to, but not over, the working lines. Be careful not to cover too large an area at one time, or the adhesive may set up before you can cover it with tile. Open times for different adhesives vary, so you'll have to experiment.

Placing the tiles. Two methods for laying out a square tile pattern are shown at right. You can use either, although it's best to use the method given in the instructions that come with the tile you're using. Method A is preferable where the open time of the

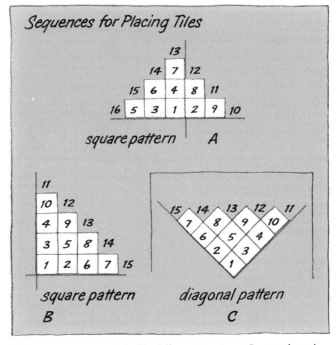

Tiling sequences: A. half of floor at a time; B. one-fourth of floor; C. one-fourth of floor for diagonal pattern.

adhesive allows you to cover a large area at a time.

Install the first tile in one of the right angles formed by the center lines. Continue laying the tiles in pyramid fashion according to method A or method B. Place each tile snugly against adjacent tiles by lining up the edges and then dropping it in place. Never slide tile into position or the adhesive will come up through the joints. Once the tile is in position, press it firmly in place. If you're using self-stick tiles, make sure the tile is positioned accurately before you press it down. These tiles are extremely hard to remove once they're fixed to the floor.

If you're installing solid vinyl or cork tiles, you'll have to bed the tiles into the adhesive with an

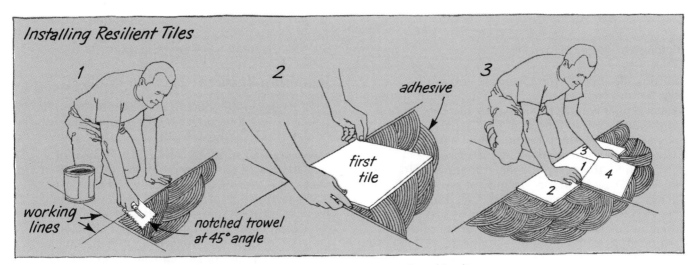

To lay tiles: *1. Spread adhesive evenly. 2. Align first tile in intersection of working lines. 3. Lay rest of tiles; match corners exactly.*

ordinary rolling pin. Do not roll vinyl-asbestos or asphalt tiles.

If you're careful not to skid on them, you can kneel on vinyl-asbestos or asphalt tiles already in position. When installing solid vinyl tiles, kneel on the subfloor (unless it's covered by adhesive) until you run out of space, then kneel on a piece of smooth plywood or hardboard (at least 2' by 2') placed over the tiles.

After you've filled in the section you're working on (half of the room for method A, one-fourth of the room for method B) with whole tiles, cut and place the border tiles in that section (see "Cutting tile," below).

For a diagonal pattern, lay out the tiles as shown in method C. The last row of tiles you lay before installing border tiles will be diagonal half tiles. If you're using tiles of contrasting colors, as shown in the drawing below, these half tiles should all be the same color.

If the tile has a pattern or grain running in one direction, cut either right or left half tiles to match the pattern or grain direction of the floor. Depending on how you cut the tile, you'll end up with either two right or two left half tiles. If one wall requires left half tiles, then the opposite wall will also have left half tiles and the two adjacent walls will have right half tiles.

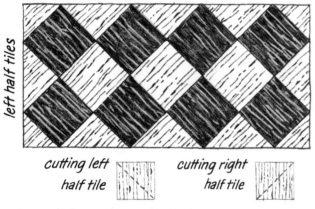

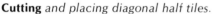

Cutting *and placing diagonal half tiles.*

Cutting tile. In addition to cutting corner tiles and border tiles to fit around the perimeter of the room, you'll probably have to make irregular cuts in some of the tiles to fit around door jambs, pipes, or other obstacles in the room. To cut asphalt and vinyl-asbestos tiles, first score along the mark with a utility knife, then snap the tile at that point. To make intricate cuts, warm the tile and cut it with a pair of heavy scissors or shears. Cut solid vinyl tiles with heavy scissors—heating helps. To heat tiles, place them in an electric oven or food warmer at a low temperature, or hold them over a heater or furnace. Be careful not to overheat the tiles—they may scorch, crack, or melt. Tiles should be warm, but not hot, to the touch.

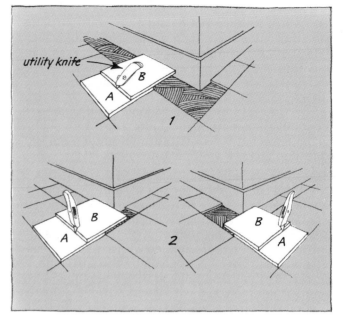

Marking border tiles: *1. against wall, 2. outside corner.*

For border tiles, position a loose tile exactly over one of the tiles in the last row (A), making sure that the grain or pattern is running in the right direction. Place another loose tile on top of the first, butting it against the wall (B). Using this tile as a guide, mark tile A with a pencil or score it with a utility knife. When cut, tile A will fit exactly in the border. Follow the same basic procedure for cutting corner tiles, as shown in the drawing above. You'll end up with an L-shaped tile.

For irregular areas, such as around a door jamb, cut a cardboard pattern to fit the space, then trace the pattern onto a tile.

Finishing touches. Once you've laid all the tiles, make a final inspection to see that they're smooth, tight, and even. Be sure that no adhesive has seeped through the joints. Remove excess adhesive from the floor surface with a rag moistened with a small amount of alcohol or the recommended solvent. Avoid getting solvent in the tile joints; it will loosen the tile. Clean all tools immediately after use.

Installing Resilient Tiles on Walls

To dress up a wall you can use any type of resilient floor tile, wood parquet tiles, or resilient tiles designed especially for walls.

Preparing wall surfaces. Wall surfaces must be prepared in the same general way as floors. First you should remove the base molding and the cover plates from electrical outlets and switches. Rough surfaces must be sanded, filled, and smoothed with the recommended patching material or trowel-on underlayment as specified by the tile manufacturer. Existing wallpaper or similar wall coverings must be removed and the subsurface primed with the recommended primer.

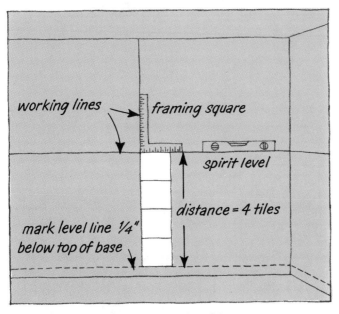

Establish *working lines with level and framing square. Install tile up and down from horizontal line.*

Walls that are below grade must first be waterproofed, then furred out and covered with a suitable backing material (your tile dealer can help you choose one). When using hardboard for backing, cement tiles to the unfinished side.

Marking the working lines. After you've prepared the wall surface and removed the base molding, check the floor along the wall to see if it's level. If it isn't, find and mark the lowest spot. Then measure up to a point ¼" less than the width of the base molding, as shown in the drawing above. From this new point, measure up the wall a distance equal to four tiles to establish the height of your horizontal working line. Using a level and chalk line, snap a level line across the wall through this point.

Next, measure and mark the midpoint of your horizontal line. Draw the vertical working line through this point as shown in the drawing. Make sure the lines intersect at 90°.

The finished wall will look better if you avoid narrow border tiles at the corners of the walls. To do this, use a tile as a guide to mark a full number of tiles from the midpoint to the corner. If the space from the last full tile to the corner is less than one-half tile, move the vertical working line over a distance of one-half tile.

Installing the tiles. Use the correct adhesive for the wall surface, as specified by the tile manufacturer. Spread only enough adhesive to install 8 to 10 tiles at a time. When applying the tiles, follow one of the methods shown on page 71 for laying floor tiles. See the preceding page for information on cutting tiles. For a job with a finished look, you can buy and install metal moldings and inside and outside metal corners. These, along with other types of molding, are available where you buy resilient tiles.

Caring for Resilient Tile

Vinyl-asbestos and solid vinyl floors with a no-wax surface can be kept clean with periodic sweeping and damp-mopping with a mild detergent or a floor cleaner sold by the manufacturer.

On these and other types of resilient floors, use only the products recommended by the manufacturer, and carefully follow instructions on their use.

Most manufacturers recommend that you refrain from washing a new floor for at least 3 days after installation. During this time, you can sweep the floor clean and remove spills with a damp cloth.

To protect the floor from indentation, remove any small metal domes or glides from furniture legs, replacing them with wide glides or furniture cups like those shown in the drawing below. Replace hard, narrow rollers with wide, soft rubber casters.

Replacing worn or damaged tiles. If your resilient floor is old enough that tiles have become worn in heavy traffic areas, you may have a hard time matching them. Even if you have some replacement tiles stashed away, new and old are bound to differ in color and thickness. If the worn tiles are confined to one area, such as that in front of a kitchen counter, you might be able to replace them by creating a design using a complementary pattern or color. Usually, though, you're better off replacing your tired old floor with new, longer-lasting resilient tiles.

With newer resilient tile floors, wear is a less frequent cause for repair than is damage—cuts, cigarette burns, furniture indentation, and so on. You'll probably have to replace only a few tiles, and most likely you will have replacements or will be able to find them easily.

To replace a damaged tile, start by removing it with a hammer and chisel. Begin in the center of the tile and work out to the edges, being careful not to damage the subfloor or surrounding tiles. Remove any excess backing or adhesive from the floor until the surface is smooth and deep enough to install the new tile. Next, apply the proper adhesive to the surface, being careful not to get any on the surrounding tiles. Finally, drop the new tile in place and press it down firmly.

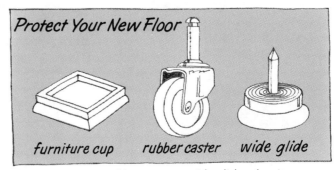

Floor protectors: *rubber casters, wide glides, furniture cups for heavy pieces.*

WOOD TILE

. . . elegance with a touch of nature

Choose wood tiles *from a large assortment of styles, wood types, and finishes. Parquets shown here typify those available for do-it-yourself installation.*

Stone

Haddon Hall

Fontainebleau

Jeffersonian

Canterbury

Finger Block

Herringbone

Parallel Finger Block

Louisville

Floors of inlaid wood mosaic—known as parquet—once graced only the mansions of the elite. Today you can enjoy the warmth and elegance of these floors at a cost comparable to that of good-quality carpeting. And you can install a parquet floor yourself with only a moderate amount of skill.

Parquet comes in the form of tiles; it is available in a variety of woods, textures, finishes, and patterns. Whether you choose a single style or create a combination, the warmth of wood will enhance the decor of any room in your home. Recreate the handsome symmetry of the floor Thomas Jefferson designed for Monticello or the elegance of Marie Antoinette's library floor at Versailles.

Parquet shouldn't be limited to floors, either. It makes an attractive, durable surface for counter and table tops. Applied to walls, parquet can add striking accents to a room. Or you can refurbish an old door with wood tiles to match the floor.

Choosing and Buying Wood Tiles

Manufacturers produce more than 100 different parquet patterns; some of the more popular ones are illustrated on the facing page. Not all patterns are available from every retailer, so you may have to shop around to find a pattern you like. In addition, you have your choice among various woods and a variety of textures, in both prefinished and unfinished tiles made of solid wood or laminated.

Woods and Finishes

Wood parquet tiles are made from many common and exotic hardwoods. You can have a parquet floor of oak, ash, walnut, pecan, or even teak. Your choice among these will depend mostly on personal taste. Tiles come either prefinished by the manufacturer or unfinished.

Prefinished wood tiles. A good choice for the amateur, prefinished tiles have their finish applied at the factory. They are available either in a natural color or stained. For instance, prefinished oak tiles range in colors from natural oak to a dark walnut and charcoal.

The factory finish usually consists of a penetrating sealer baked into the wood, followed by a coat of hot-melt wax. The result is a durable surface that will give long wear if properly maintained.

Unfinished wood tiles. Used by most professional floorlayers, unfinished tiles are less expensive than the prefinished kind, but require more work to finish after initial installation. They'll need sanding, scraping, filling (in some cases), staining, and finishing. It's best to have a professional do the sanding. The finishing processes are a lot of work, but they result in a beautiful, smooth surface. The joints between unfinished tiles can be treated with a sealer against moisture—an advantage in areas that may get wet. (The waxy surface of prefinished tiles tends to repel sealers, making the moisture-sealing of joints a difficult task.) Another plus is that unfinished wood tiles offer many more parquet patterns than the prefinished variety.

Consider Surface Texture

Although smooth parquet floors are frequently a favored choice, some manufacturers offer wood tiles with rough textures that afford an informal or rustic effect. A distressed or weathered surface gives a feeling of antiquity. Tiles with a rough-sawn surface are a good choice for a rustic atmosphere. Some tiles are wire brushed before finishing at the factory: the bristles remove the soft sapwood from the surface, producing a relief texture ideal for an informal decor.

Types of Wood Tiles

Modern wood tiles come in two forms: solid wood and laminated (plywood) tiles. Both types are available with square or tongue-and-groove edges, depending on pattern, thickness, and manufacturer (see drawing on page 76).

Common tile sizes range from 4" square to 16" square with thicknesses from 5/16" to ¾". Some of the more intricate patterns come in panels as large as 39" on a side. You can also buy rectangular tiles, as well as reducer strips to finish off the edge of the parquet floor in a door opening.

(Continued on next page)

... Continued from page 75

Solid Wood Tiles. These tiles actually consist of several pieces of solid wood (see drawing below). If the individual pieces are large, they are held together with splines of wood, metal, or plastic. Tiles composed of many small pieces—such as most mosaic patterns—have a cotton or plastic mesh on the back to hold the pieces in position until the tile is laid. Solid wood tiles are not recommended on floors below grade or in locations where moisture could be a problem.

Laminated tiles. To produce laminated wood tiles, three or more layers of hardwood are bonded together with waterproof glue, under pressure, at a high temperature. The grain of each layer runs perpendicular to that of the adjoining layers (see drawing below). This laminated, cross-grain construction makes the tiles very stable; they are preferred for use in areas where moisture could cause swelling, warping, or movement in the floor.

The Advantages of Wood

Visual appeal isn't the only reason for considering wood tile. Modern factory-applied finishes are so tough and durable that they may outlast the mortgage. Even if heavy traffic wears through the finish, you can refinish the floor for a fraction of the cost of replacing other flooring materials. You can repair wood tile without having to replace it as you must with other kinds of tile. And wood tiles are just as easy to install as resilient tiles (see page 69). To make the job even easier, some tiles come with self-stick adhesive on the back.

Wood is a warm material not only in appearance, but underfoot as well. It feels warmer than any other flooring material except carpeting—an important quality if bare feet are common around your house. The insulating qualities of wood also result in some saving of energy.

Buying What You Need

Calculate the floor area to be covered by measuring the length and width in feet and multiplying the two quantities. The answer is the area in square feet. If your room has an irregular shape, divide it into rectangles. Calculate the area of each and add the quantities together to find the total areas (see page 68). Add 5 percent to the total area to cover cutting waste and future replacement if a tile is ever damaged beyond repair.

Depending upon the size and type of tile you buy, a box of wood tiles will cover from 25 to 55 square feet. If the dealer stocks the pattern you choose, you can probably break a box and buy the exact number of tiles required. Should you have to order the tiles specially from a distributor, you may have to purchase full boxes. If you have tiles left over, consider covering a larger area or using the surplus to cover a table or a counter top.

Ask the dealer which mastic the manufacturer recommends and how much you will need. If the surface you are covering is porous or dusty, the manufacturer may recommend that it be primed; in that case, buy both the mastic and the primer when you purchase the tiles.

Tools You Will Need

Most of the tools you will need are general-purpose ones you may already have: folding rule or steel tape, claw hammer, putty knife, square, rubber mallet, chalk line, and crosscut saw or electric saber saw. The saber saw is ideal for cutting the wood tile to irregular shapes to fit around obstructions. You will probably have to buy a special notched trowel to spread the adhesive. The tile manufacturer usually specifies the trowel requirements.

To bed the tiles into the adhesive, some manufacturers recommend that you use a 150-pound

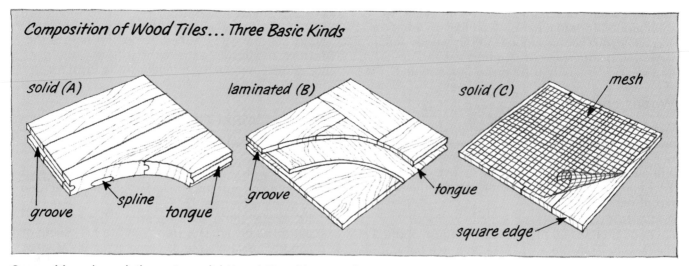

Composition of wood tiles varies: solid (A and C) and laminated (B). Both come with either tongue-and-groove or square edges. Splines or mesh fasten hardwood pieces to form solid wood tiles; layers of wood are glued in laminated construction.

floor roller; most tool rental shops will have one. A roller is especially helpful if you have a large area to cover. To avoid damage to the parquet surface, be sure the roller is covered with a resilient material and that it is clean.

If you choose to install unfinished wood tiles and to sand and finish the floor yourself, you will need a floor sander and an edger. (The edger is a sanding machine designed to sand the floor close to the walls where the floor sander can't reach.) Most tool rental shops stock these two items as well. **Use great caution when operating these machines:** you can easily gouge the floor with them, causing nearly irreparable damage. Practice on an old floor or a sheet of plywood until you get the feel of both sanders.

How to Install Parquet

Laying a parquet floor is not an extremely complicated job, but it does require careful planning and preparation. The job has two stages: preparation of the surface on which the tile will be laid and actual placement of the tiles.

A properly prepared subfloor will help you achieve a better-quality, longer-lasting parquet floor. Careful measurement and placement of the tiles will insure even patterns and regular alignment of the tiles from one end of the room to the other.

Whether tiles are unfinished or prefinished, the method of laying them is generally the same. However, read carefully the manufacturer's instructions enclosed with each box of tiles.

Preparing the Surface

You can install parquet over subfloors of concrete, wood plank, or plywood, as well as over finish wood floors. Whatever the surface, start by removing all base and shoe moldings, door thresholds, and any doors that swing into the room. If you have an existing resilient floor, you probably have only two choices: remove it or cover it up. Both options are described in the chapter on resilient tile (see page 69).

Old wood floors or subfloors. If the subfloor planks or the strips or tiles of the previous finish floor are loose or bowed, renail them. Remove any high spots by rough-sanding; if they're widespread, use a floor sander. You must remove any shellac, varnish, paint, lacquer, or wax from old finish floors; rough-sanding with a floor sander is the easiest way.

If the planks in your floor are too badly bowed to flatten by nailing or sanding, you'll have to install underlayment panels over them (see page 70). If the planks are 4" wide or less, you can cover them with ¼"-thick untempered hardboard, rough side up, or plywood. For planks from 4" to 6"

wide, use ⅜" plywood; for planks over 6" wide, ⅝" plywood is best.

Fasten ¼" or ⅜" material with 3-penny ring shank or 4-penny cement-coated nails. Fasten ⅝" plywood with 4-penny ring shank or 5-penny cement-coated nails. Space the nails 6" apart across the surface of the panels.

Concrete floors. Moisture is a serious concern if you're installing wood tiles over a concrete floor. Excessive moisture coming up through the concrete can cause wood tiles to swell, buckle, or even rot. See page 45 for details on testing a concrete floor for moisture.

A concrete subfloor must be in good condition (free of cracks, smooth, and clean) before tiles can be installed. To remove grease and oil stains, you can use a chemical garage floor cleaner available from most auto supply stores. Chip or scrape off any excess concrete, globs of paint, or other foreign material. If the floor was sealed or painted, sand it down to bare concrete with a floor sander and #4 or #5 open-cut sandpaper. Remove high spots by rubbing with a coarse grade of abrasive stone. Finish the preparation by scouring with a stiff-bristle or wire brush and vacuuming up all loose material.

As a final step, fill low areas, cracks, holes, and expansion joints in the concrete with a mastic underlayment or a good concrete patching material. If your floor is rough or uneven, you may find it easier to have a contractor pour a new slab over the old one or install a plywood subfloor on sleepers.

Laying the Floor

Once you've prepared the subfloor, you're ready to lay the wood tiles. You will need to plan the placement, establish your working lines, and have the proper adhesive ready to spread.

Before installing the wood tiles, you must acclimate them to the humidity and temperature of the room. Remove the tiles from the boxes and spread them out on the floor. Leave the tiles for 72 hours, then stack them at convenient spots in the room.

Marking the working lines. Refer to the layout method for a square pattern on pages 70–71, or the one recommended by the manufacturer. Select the one that best suits your situation and use it to mark your working lines. If the room has several openings or if the walls are badly bowed or out of square, arrange the working lines to minimize the visual effect of these on the finished floor.

Spreading the adhesive. If the adhesive manufacturer recommends priming the surface, now is the time to do it.

Read the instructions on the adhesive container, paying particular attention to the open time (see page 71); plan your work accordingly. If you primed the surface, make certain the primer is dry before going on to the next step.

(Continued on page 79)

Installing Wood Tiles . . . Step-by-Step

Step 1. Spread adhesive with notched trowel. Do not cover working lines.

Step 2. Lay first tile. Align edges carefully with intersection of working lines.

Step 3. Place next three tiles. Match corners exactly; butt edges together tightly.

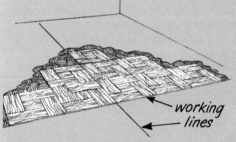

Step 4. Install tiles across room, maintaining step pattern and tile alignment.

Step 5. Strike tiles with rubber mallet to bed them firmly into adhesive.

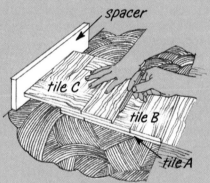

Step 6. Set tile B for border exactly atop last full tile A. Set tile C against spacer; mark cutting line on tile B.

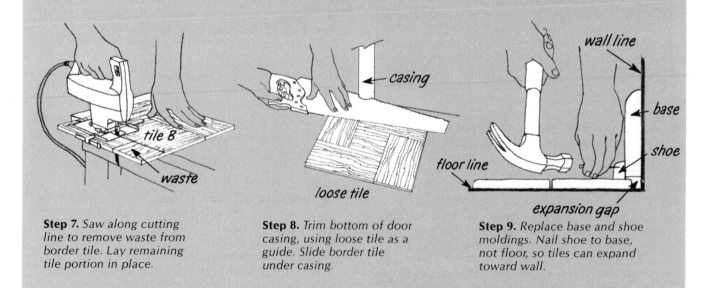

Step 7. Saw along cutting line to remove waste from border tile. Lay remaining tile portion in place.

Step 8. Trim bottom of door casing, using loose tile as a guide. Slide border tile under casing.

Step 9. Replace base and shoe moldings. Nail shoe to base, not floor, so tiles can expand toward wall.

. . . Continued from page 77

Using a putty knife, transfer some of the adhesive from the container onto the floor at the spot where you will lay the first tile. Holding the notched trowel at a 45° angle to the floor, spread the adhesive with firm pressure on the trowel (see step 1 on the facing page). You should be able to see your chalked working lines between the ribbons of the adhesive. If you can't, spread the adhesive up to but not over the working lines.

Placing the tiles. At last you're ready to put the tiles on the floor. Here are some pointers:

• Follow the tile placement sequence below or the one suggested by the manufacturer. This will maintain a step pattern as you work across the room. In this way each new tile will be laid against a corner, making it easier to maintain alignment.

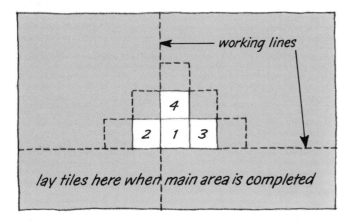

• Work carefully. Make certain that the corners of each tile are lined up perfectly with those adjoining.

• After you spread the adhesive, keep it clean and don't walk on it.

• If you *must* walk or kneel on freshly laid tile, lay down some pieces of plywood first in order to distribute your weight. Otherwise the tiles may slide out of position or the adhesive may be forced up into the joints.

Place the first tile at the intersection of your two working lines (see step 2). Carefully align the edges —not the tongues—with the lines. The care with which you lay the first 10 tiles will determine the alignment and appearance of the whole floor. A small error here can magnify to a misalignment of inches by the time you reach the wall.

Set the second tile, as shown on the pattern above, against the first one; align it carefully with both the first tile and the working line. If the tiles are the tongue-and-groove variety, engage them as you put the second tile in place. Don't slide the tiles in place any more than absolutely necessary. Excessive sliding will push the adhesive into the joints between the tiles, causing misalignment.

Set the third and fourth tiles with the same care (see step 3). Continue laying tiles, maintaining the sawtooth pattern shown in step 4, as you work toward the walls. After you've set several tiles, strike

them sharply with a rubber mallet to bed them into the adhesive (see step 5). Clean any adhesive off the surface of the tiles as you go along, using small amounts of the thinner suggested on the adhesive container.

When you reach a wall, you will probably need to cut tiles to fit. A ½" to ¾" gap between the last tile and the wall is necessary to allow for the natural expansion of the wood tiles. Some manufacturers supply a cork expansion strip; use this material, when it is available, to fill the gap. To fit a border tile, mark it as shown in step 6. The thickness of the piece of wood between the top tile and the wall will determine the width of the expansion gap you leave. Use your crosscut or saber saw to cut the tile (see step 7). Cut and set the border tiles as you . proceed.

At each doorway, use a tile for a guide to cut off the bottom of the casing (see step 8). Then install the tile by sliding it underneath the end of the casing. Your parquet floor should end under the door. You can use a prefinished reducer strip to finish off the edge or a wood saddle to cover it.

Finishing the job. Let the adhesive dry overnight, and then replace the base and shoe moldings (see step 9). Nail the shoe to the base—if you nail it to the floor, the wood tiles may not be able to expand and the floor may buckle. Rehang the doors. If a door does not clear the new parquet floor, remove it and cut some material off the bottom of the door.

Caring for the New Floor

A few simple procedures will help maintain the beauty of your parquet floor. Hardwood is one of the easiest floors to maintain and one of the few floors that can be repaired when damaged.

Periodic care. A good paste wax—not a water-based wax—will give added protection to the wood. Buff about twice a year; wax about once a year. Excessive waxing can cause wax to build up, detracting from the floor's appearance.

Day-to-day care. Dust-mop or vacuum your parquet floor as you would carpeting. Do not scrub or wet-mop the parquet. Use a damp cloth to remove fresh food spills.

Repair and restoration. Some manufacturers of prefinished wood tiles offer renovation kits. These contain the materials and instructions needed to repair minor damage such as wear marks and stains.

Most manufacturers can supply you with methods for removing white spots, water marks, dark (or dog) spots, ink stains, and grease marks. If a tile is badly damaged, replace it as follows:

Set the blade depth of a circular saw to the tile thickness. Make a cut near each edge of the damaged tile (don't cut into the adjoining ones) and chisel it out. Remove the groove bottoms from the new tile, spread mastic on the back and slip it into place.

INDEX

GLOSSARY

Backing. 1) Any material used as a foundation for ceramic tile. 2) The underside of a resilient or wood tile.

Backsplash. The wall area covered with ceramic tile behind or around a sink or counter.

Base. 1) A flat wood molding used at the bottom of a wall to finish off a floor. Sometimes called base mold or molding. 2) *See* Backing, definition 1.

Batten. Wood strip usually 1″ by 2″ or 1″ by 3.″

Body. Structural portion of a ceramic tile as opposed to the finished top surface.

Bone pile. Stock of defective tiles and custom-order overruns maintained by some tile manufacturers; usually sold at a substantial discount.

Buttering. Spreading a thin coat of adhesive on the back of a tile just before placing it.

Chalk line. 1) String, coated with chalk, used to mark reference lines on a work surface. 2) The mark made on a working surface by snapping a stretched chalk line.

Culinarios. Traditional name for handpainted folk tiles.

Fume. To create an iridescent effect on ceramic tile by exposing the molten glaze to chemical fumes.

Furring. Wood strips used to build out a wall surface.

Glaze. Hard, glassy coating fused to the top surface of a ceramic tile by firing at a high temperature.

Grade. Ground level; floors are classified as above-grade, on-grade, or below-grade.

Hand-decorated. *See* Handpainted.

Handpainted. Decorative glaze applied to a ceramic tile by hand with a brush.

Kickplate. Bottom of counter recessed for toe space.

Leg. Narrow column of ceramic tiles on the walls in front of a bathtub.

Mosaic. 1) Small ceramic tiles arranged in a pattern and joined into sheets by cotton or paper mesh, or by dabs of silicone rubber. 2) Intricate pattern formed with small ceramic tiles or pieces of ceramic tile, wood, glass, or stone.

Open time. Period of time during which an adhesive retains its ability to stick to a tile and bond it to a backing.

Parquet. 1) Floor made with an inlaid mosaic of wood. 2) A wood tile composed of several pieces of wood arranged in a pattern.

Receptor. Waterproof base for a shower.

Scraffito. A technique for decorating ceramic tile by cutting through the glaze before firing to expose the tile body.

Seconds. Tiles with minor defects of glaze, color, or form. Usually sold at a substantial discount.

Sleepers. Lengths of lumber fastened to a concrete floor to support a wood subfloor.

Splines. Thin wood, metal, or plastic strips on the underside of a wood tile that hold the individual pieces of wood together.

Stoneware. Type of high-temperature-fired ceramic body with red spots of iron pulled to the surface by the temperature.

Terra cotta. 1) An inexpensive, low-temperature-fired ceramic tile. 2) A color, brownish orange.

Tesserae. Very small, square, individual ceramic tiles. *See also* Mosaic.

Trompe l'oeil. Decorated surface that creates an illusion of reality.

Underlayment. Material used to smooth and level irregularities in subfloors. Underlayments include plywood, particle board (if made specifically for this purpose), hardboard, and several types of pliable coatings.

Wainscot. A facing such as ceramic, resilient, or wood tile applied to the lower part of a wall.